MERMAID
Coloring Book
FOR KIDS ~ AGE 4-12

Copyright © 2020 Kenzth Art
All rights reserved.
ISBN: 9798654342911

This Book Belongs To

_____

Color Swatch
Test your color here !

Before beginning to color, please place a blank page behind each one, to prevent bleed-trough to the next page.

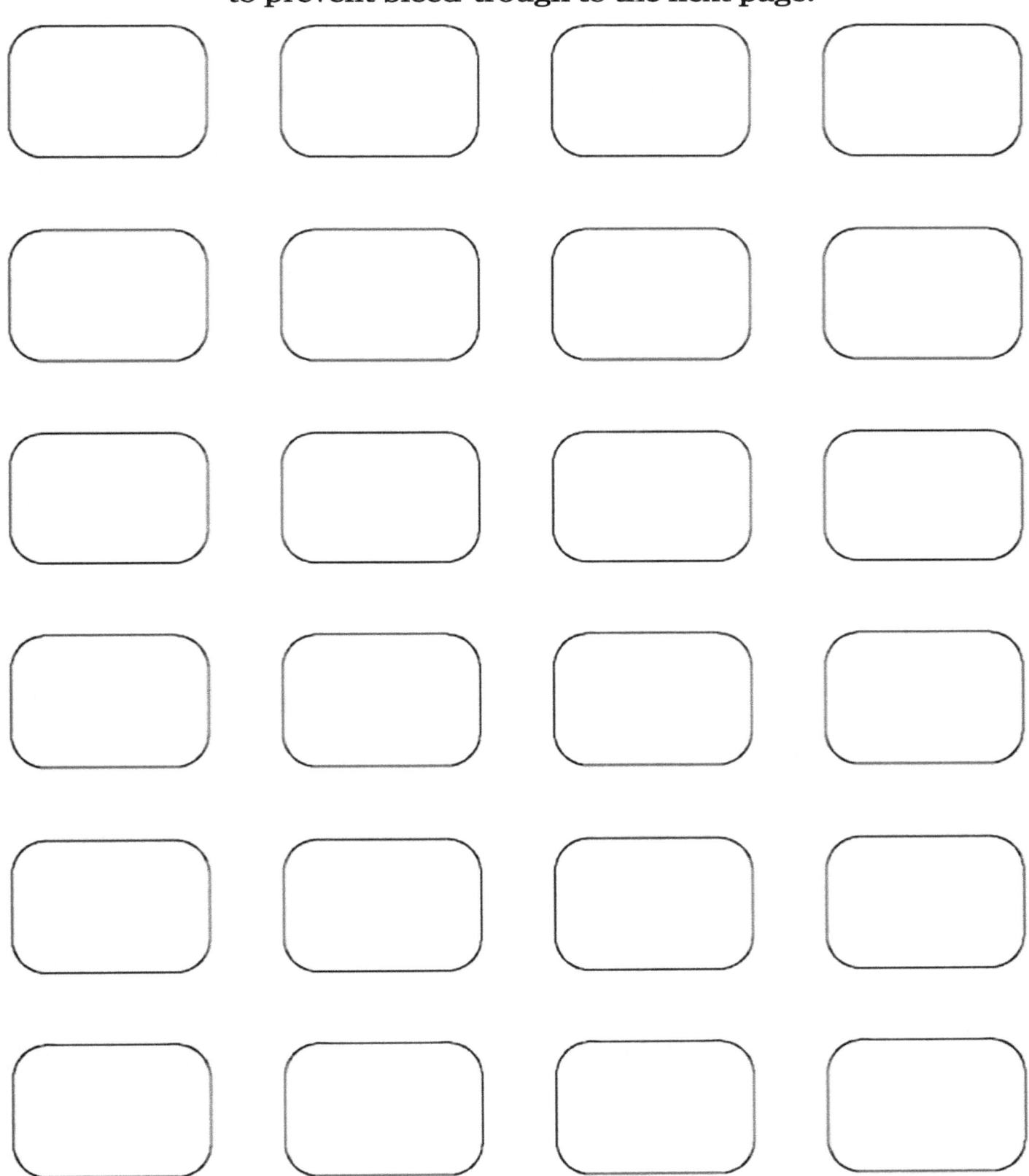

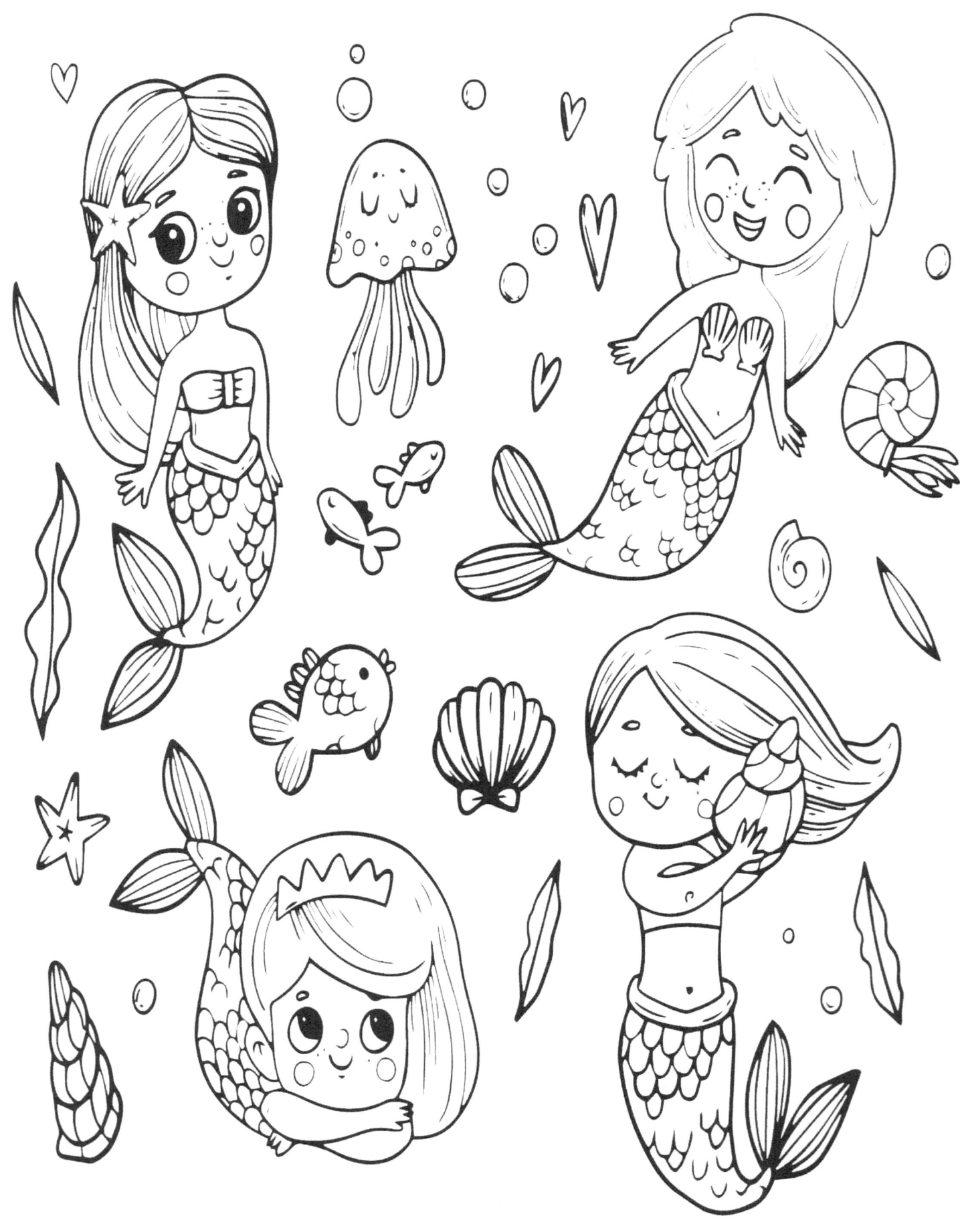

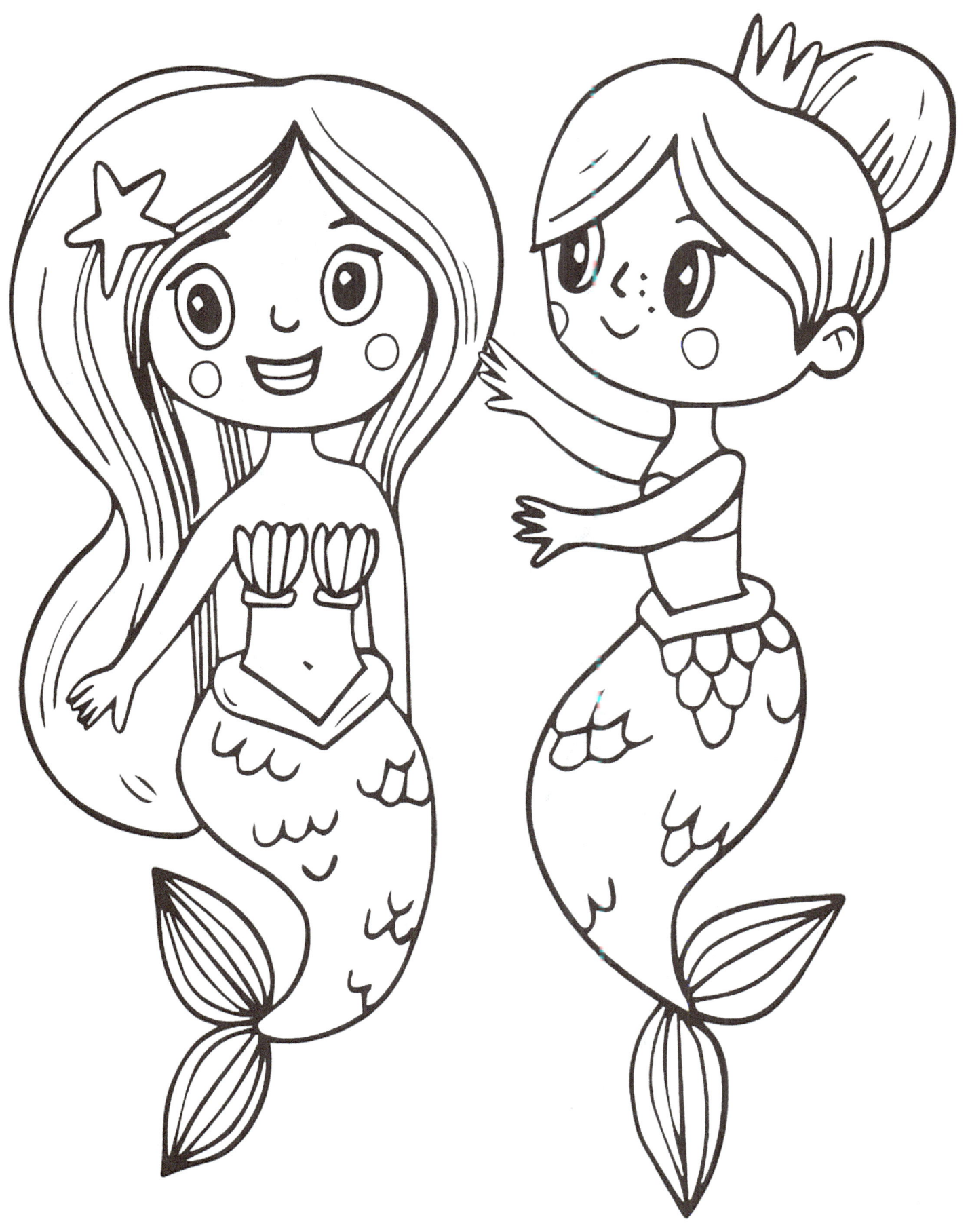

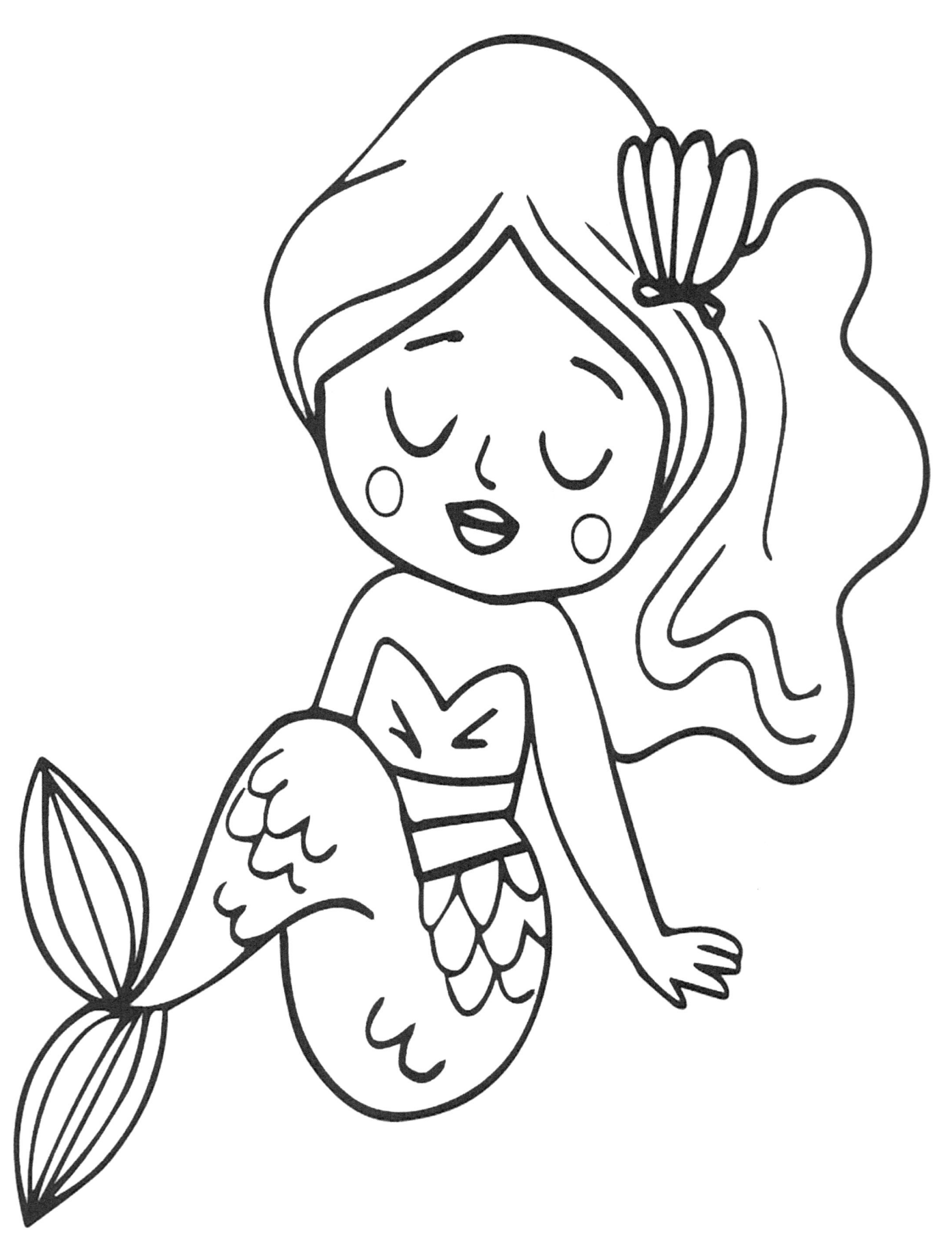

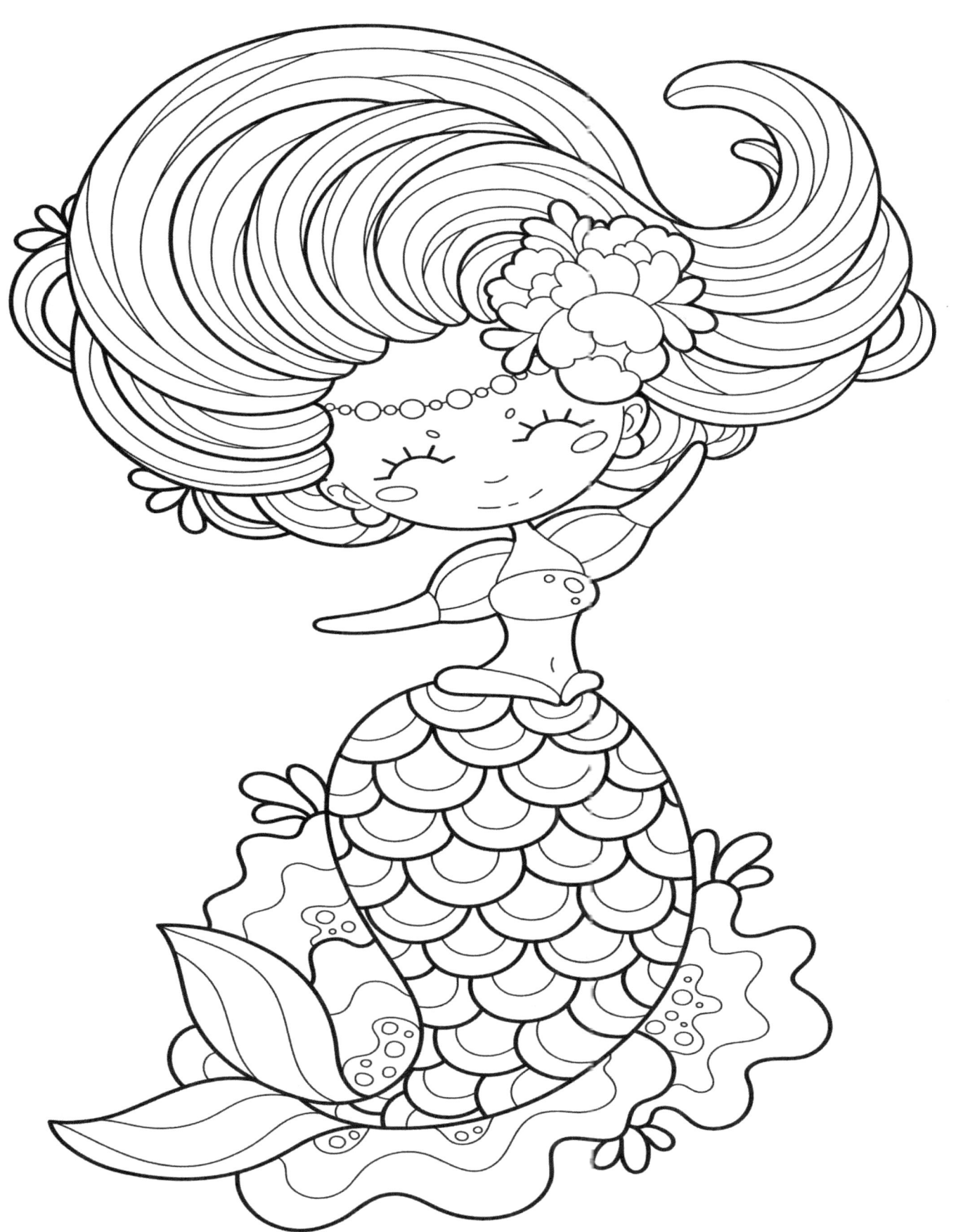

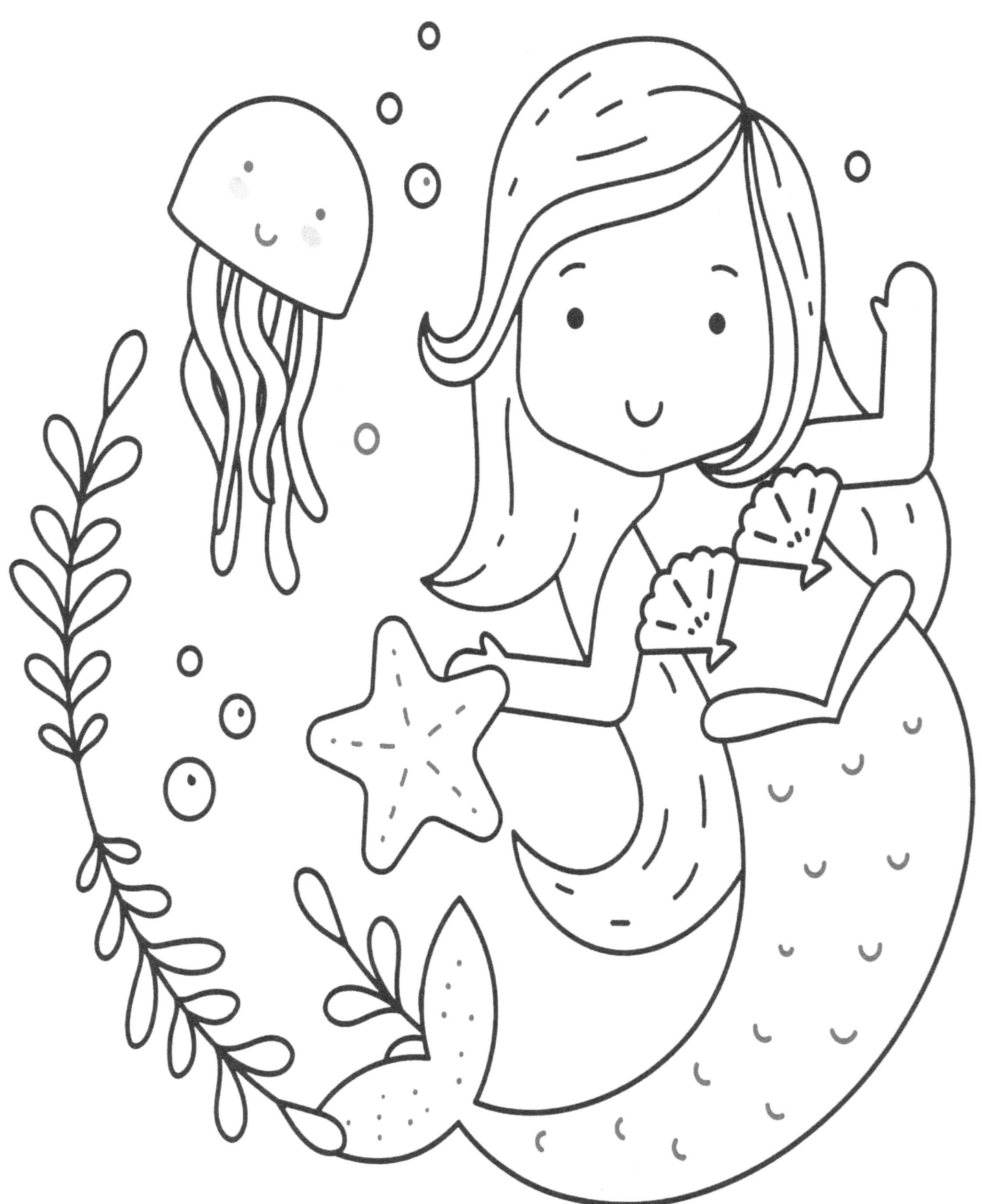

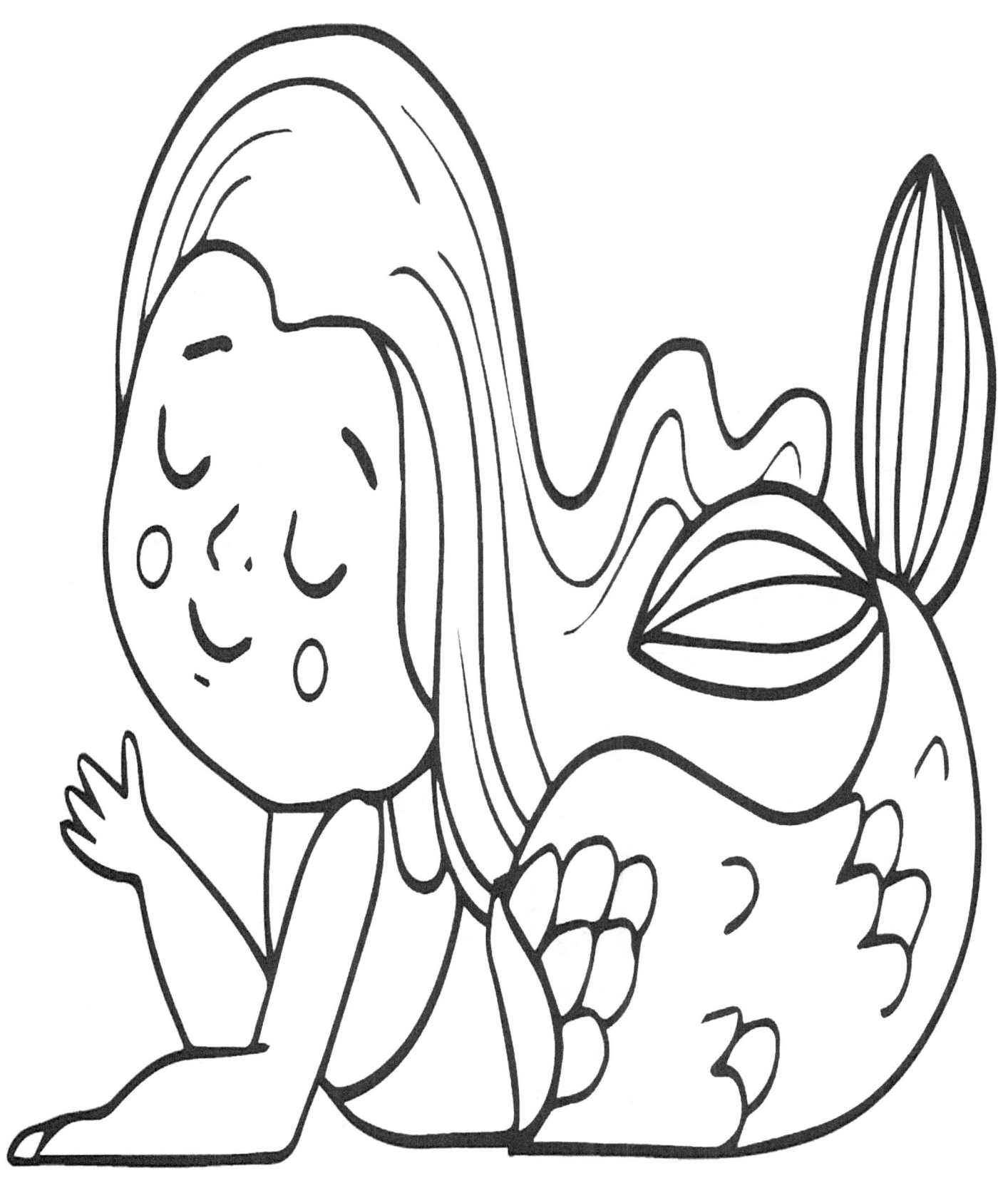

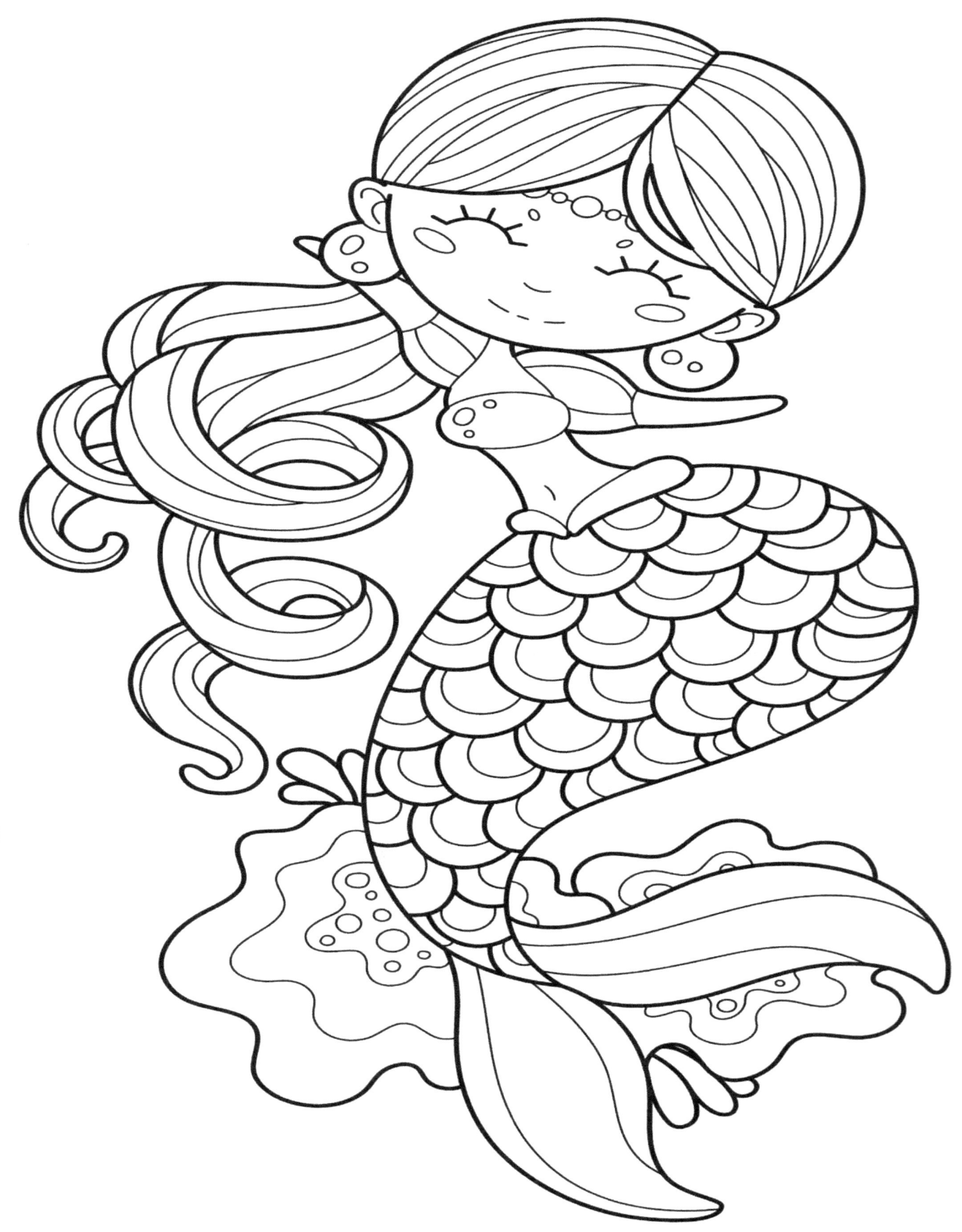

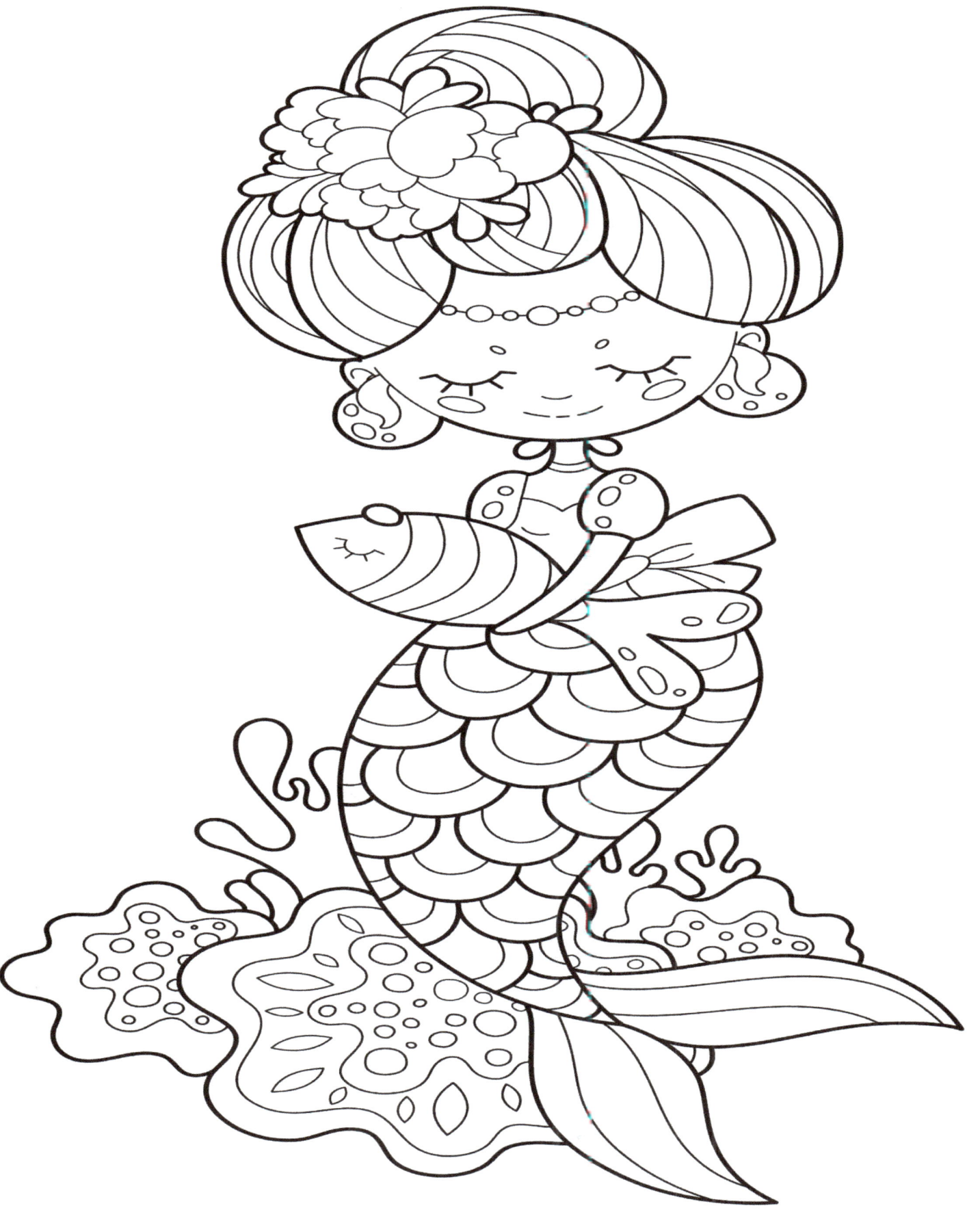

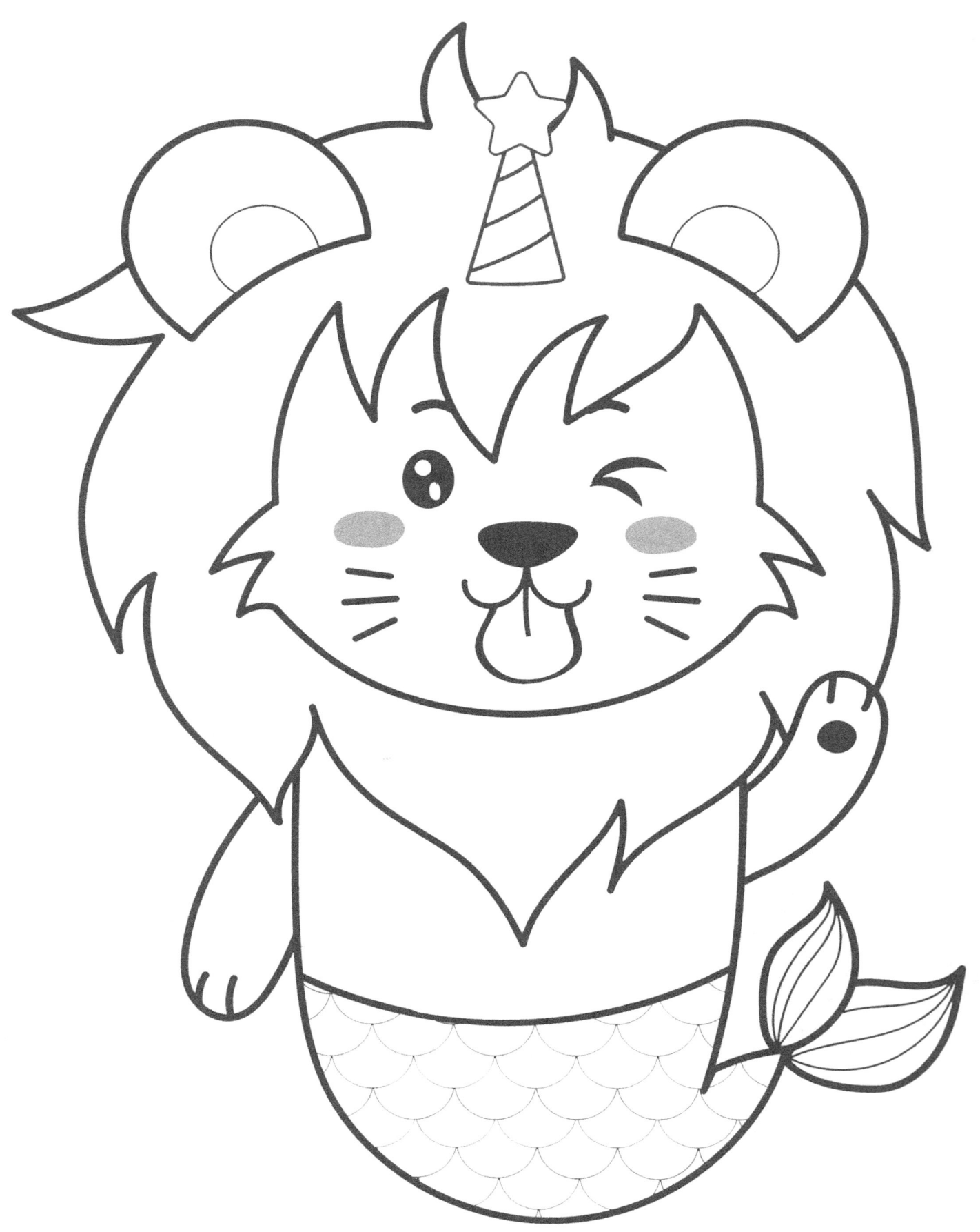

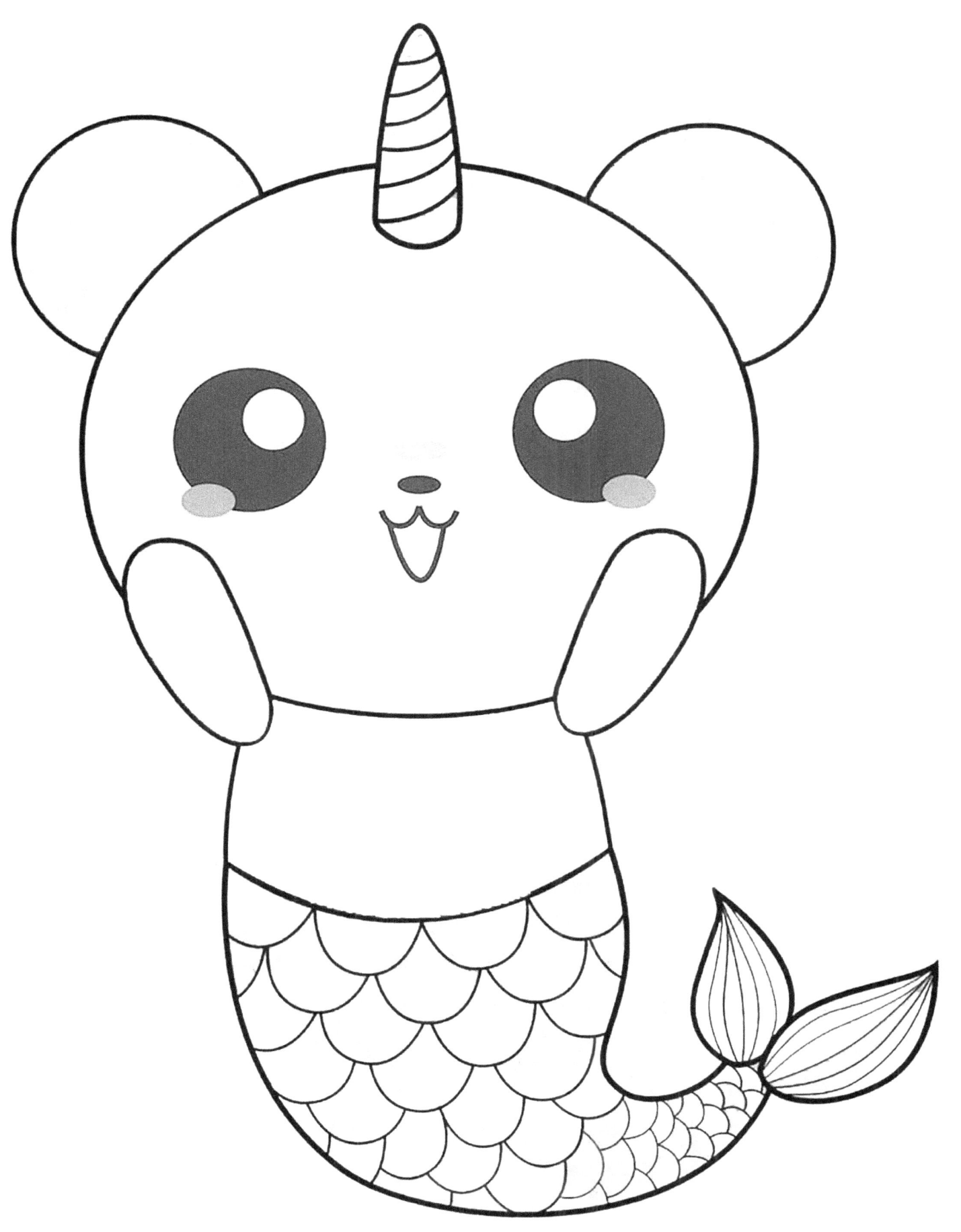

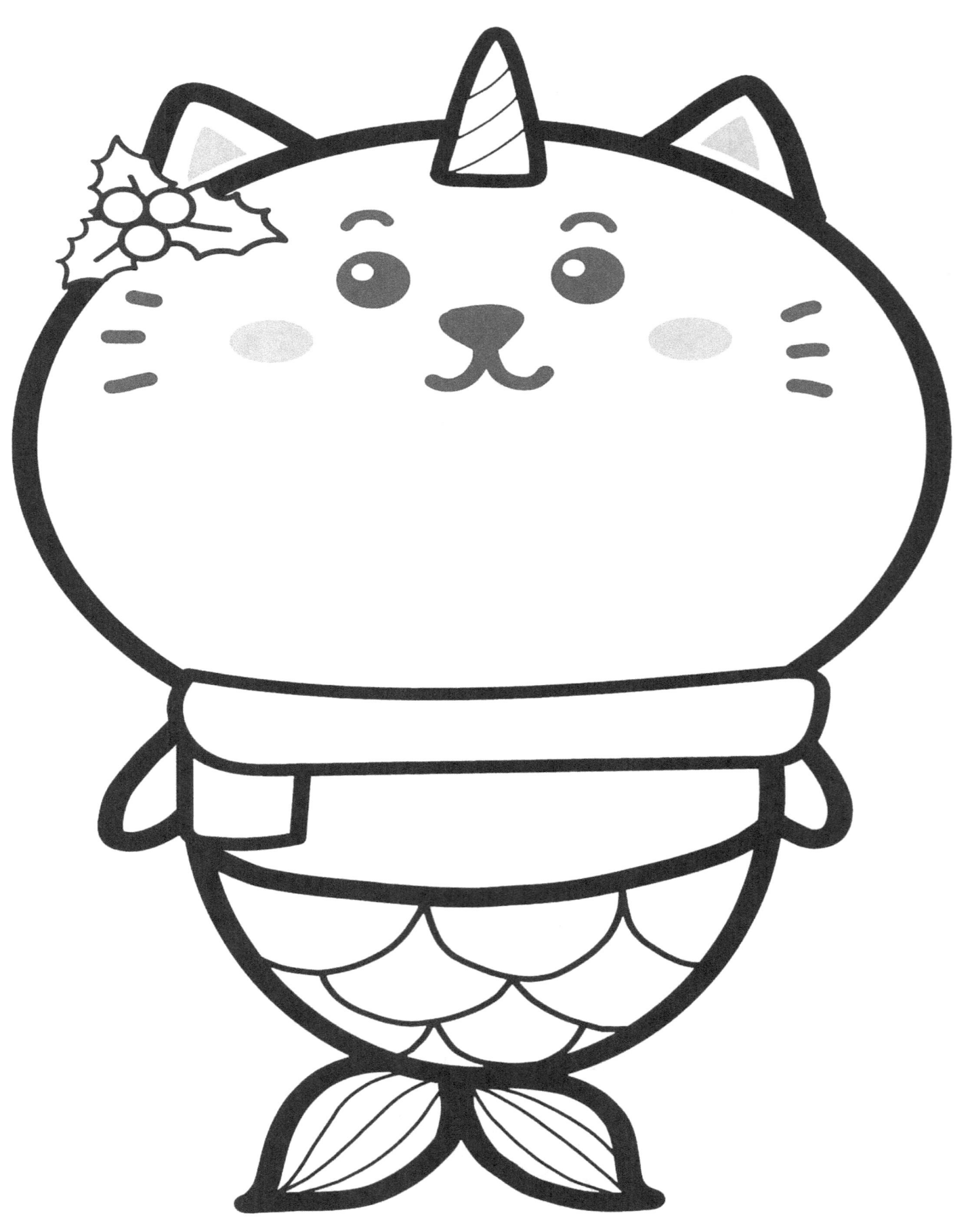

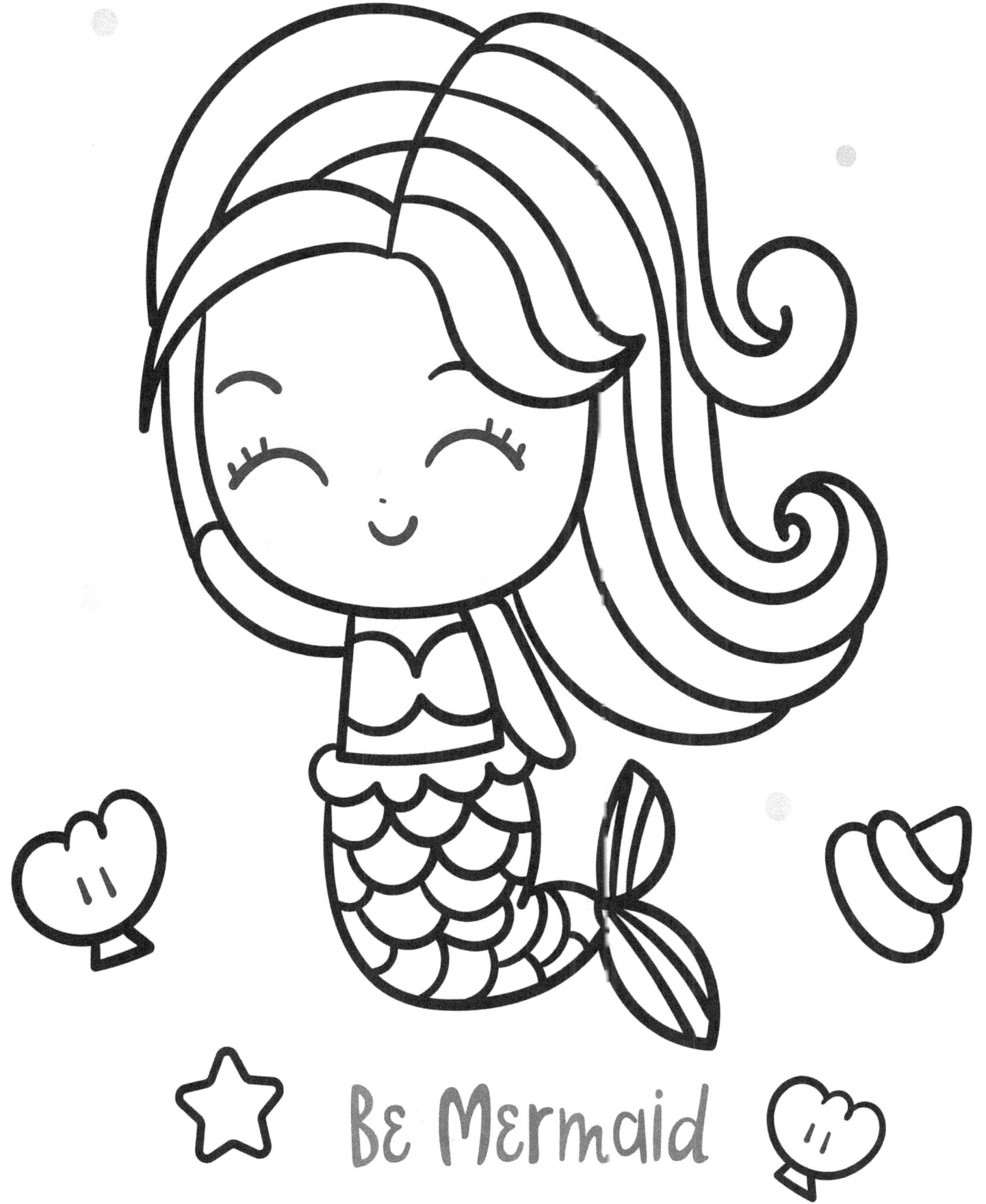

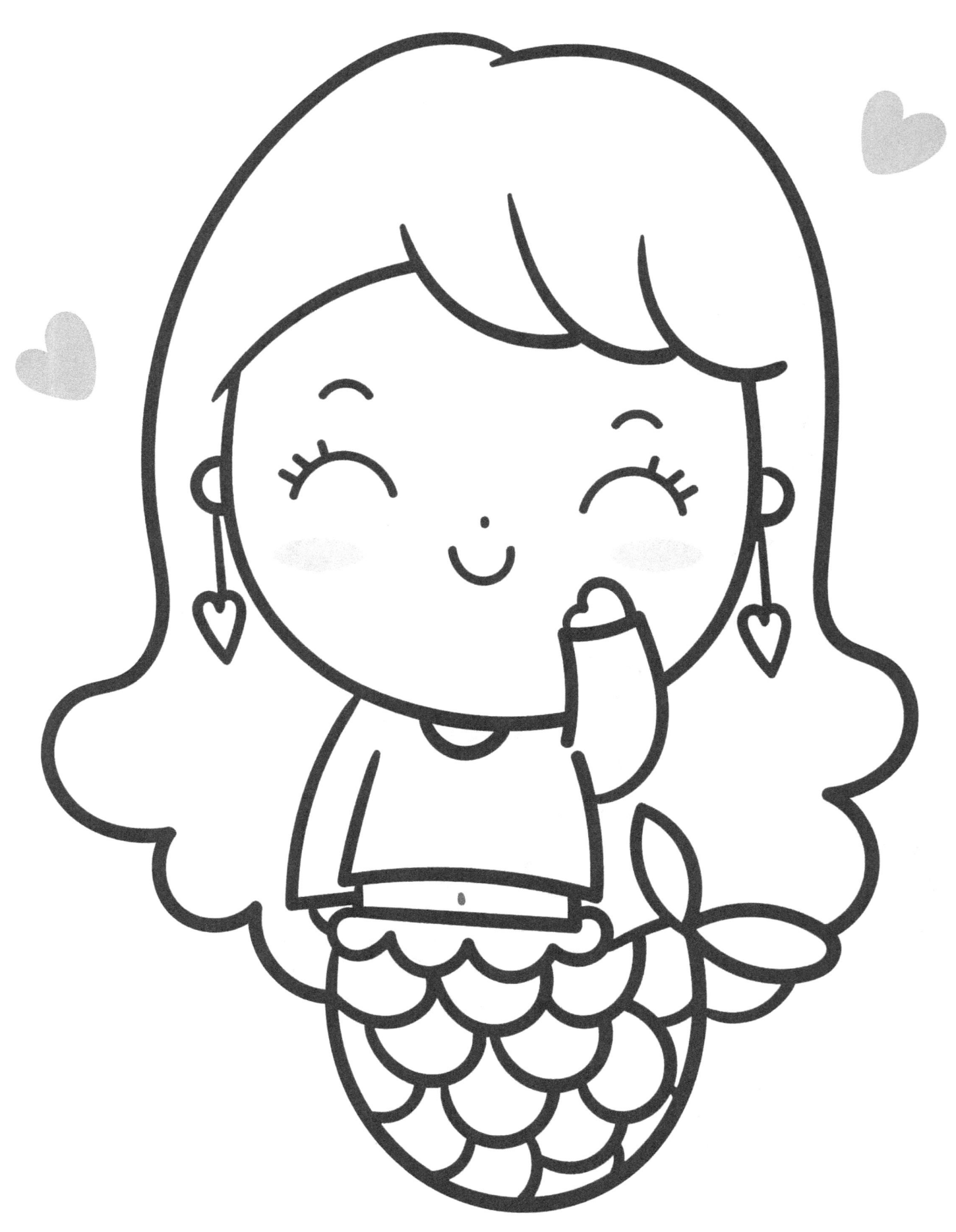

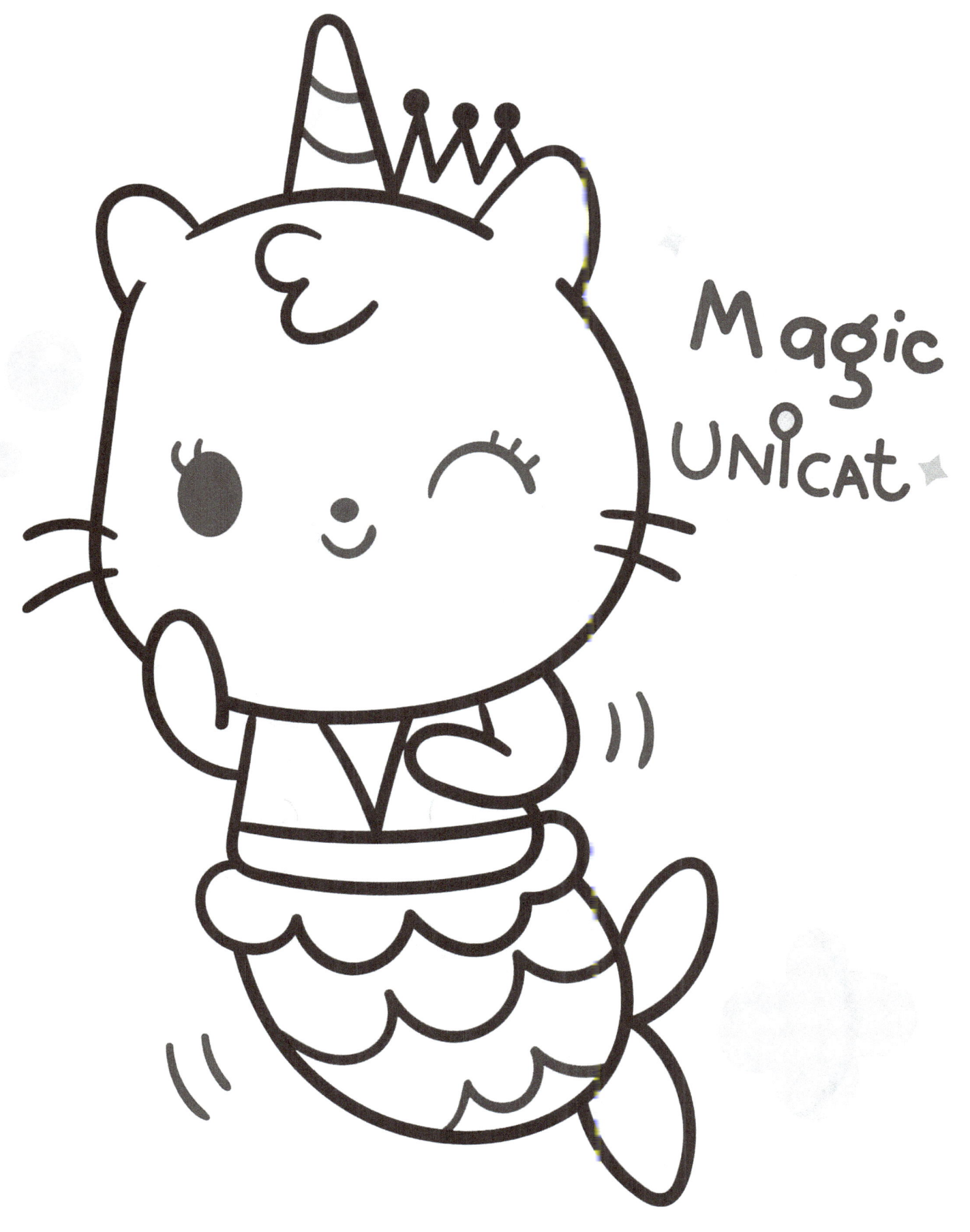

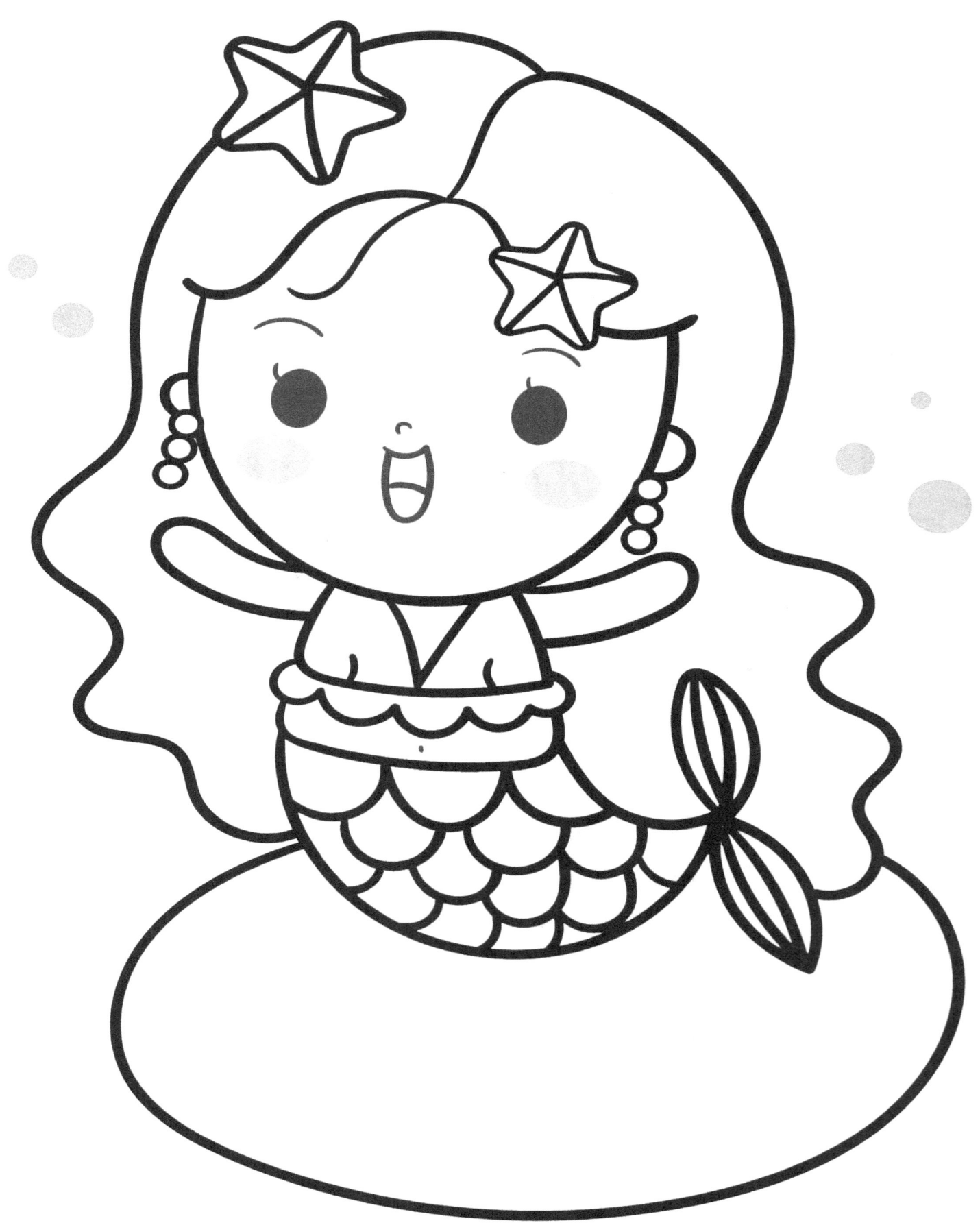

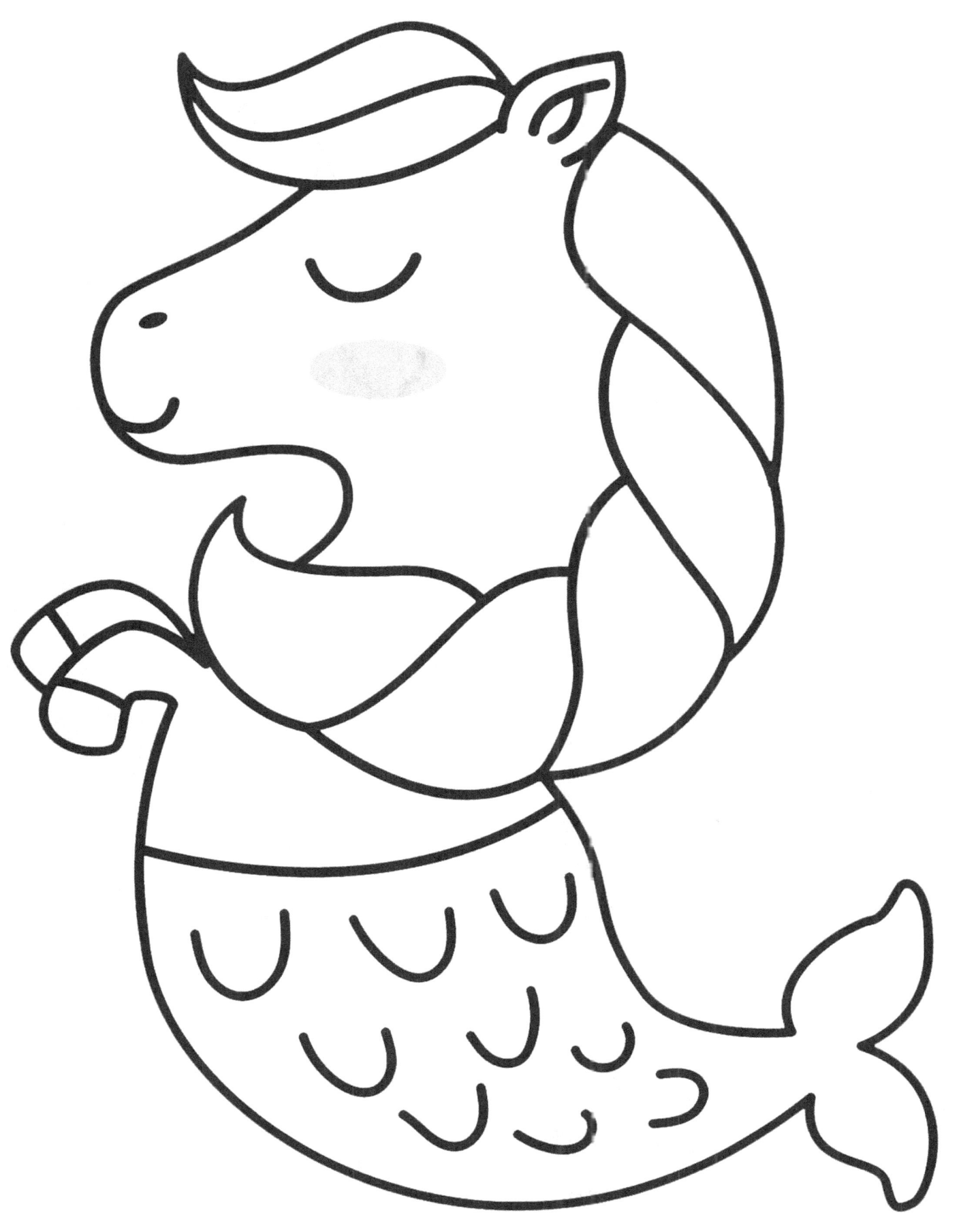

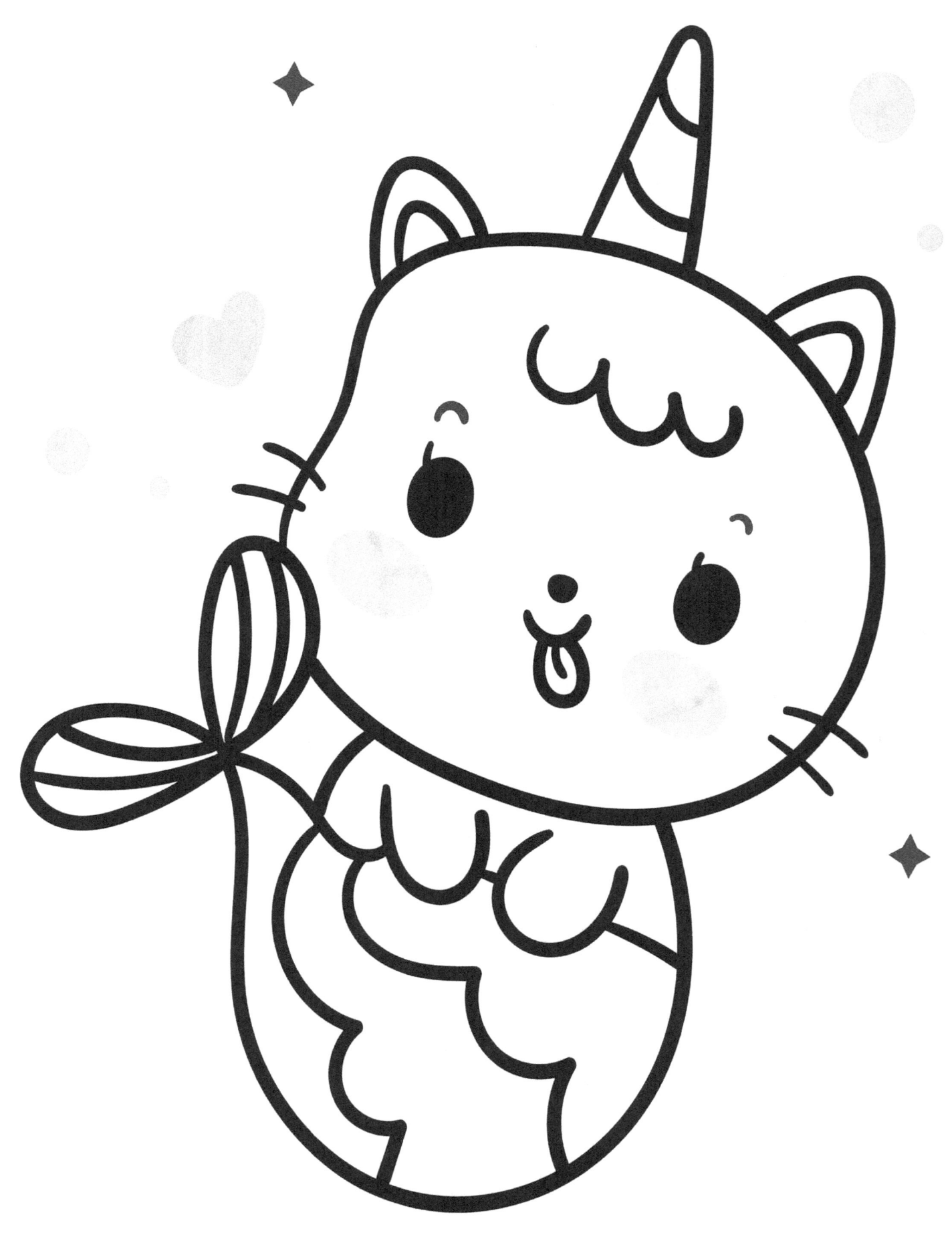

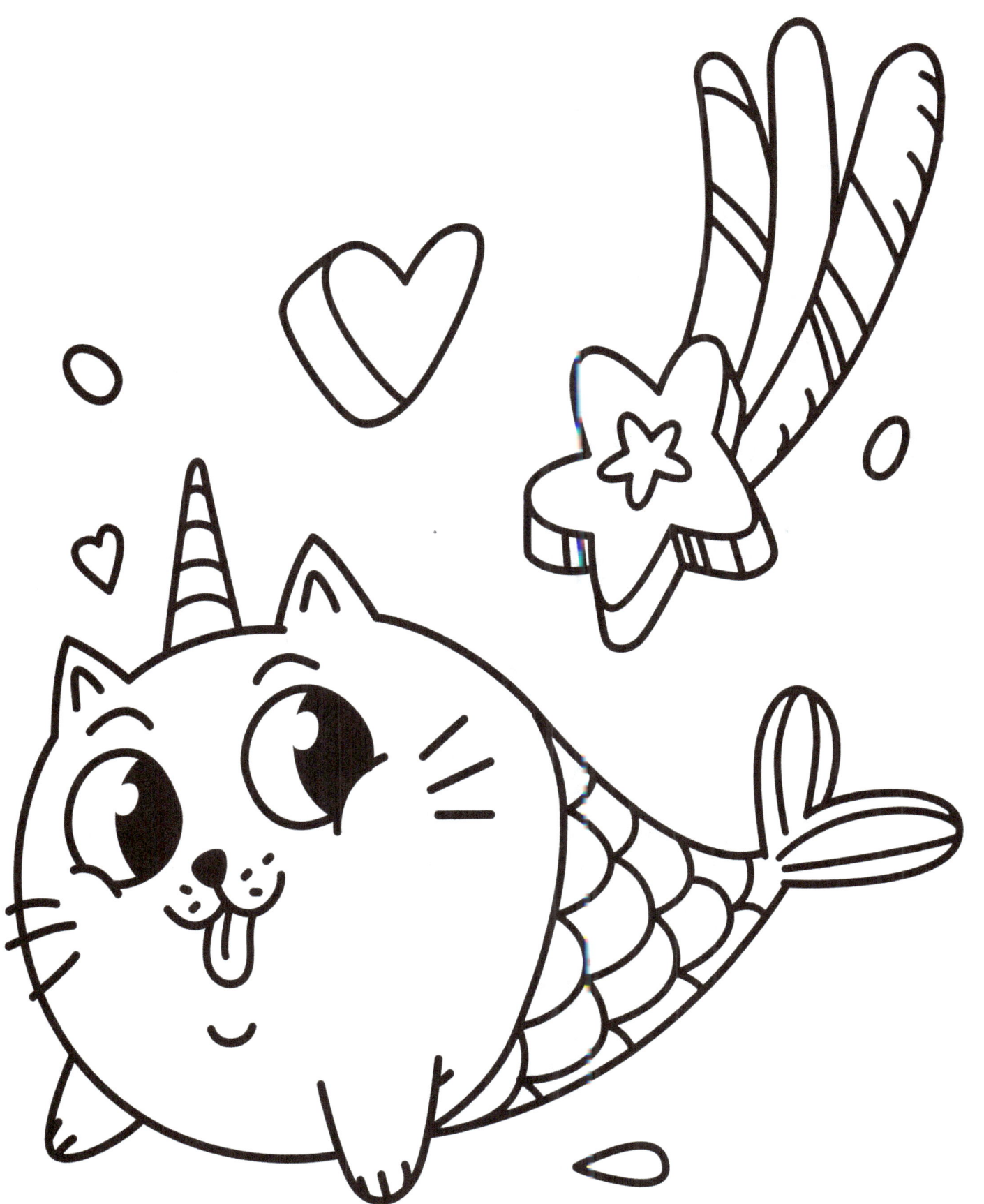

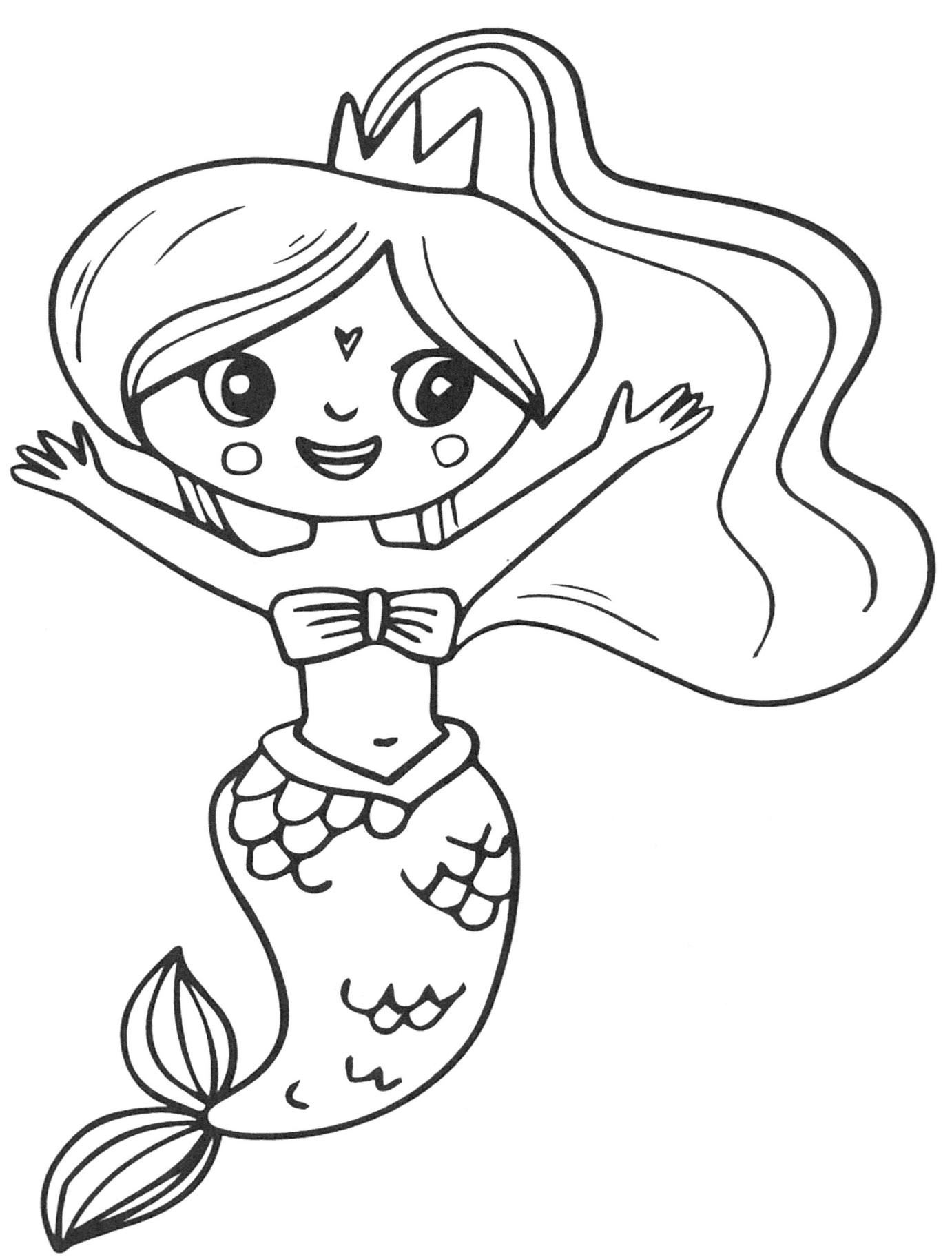

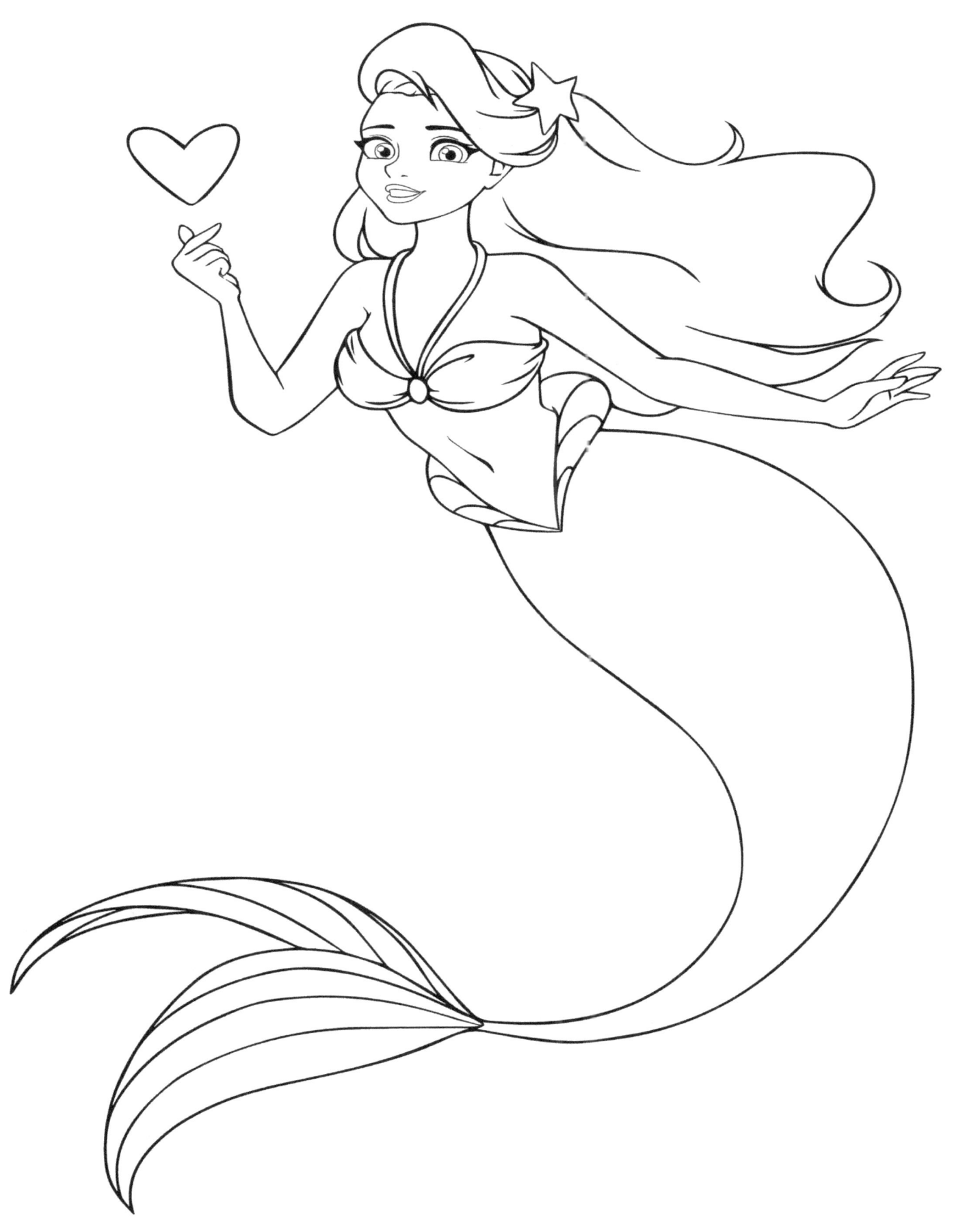

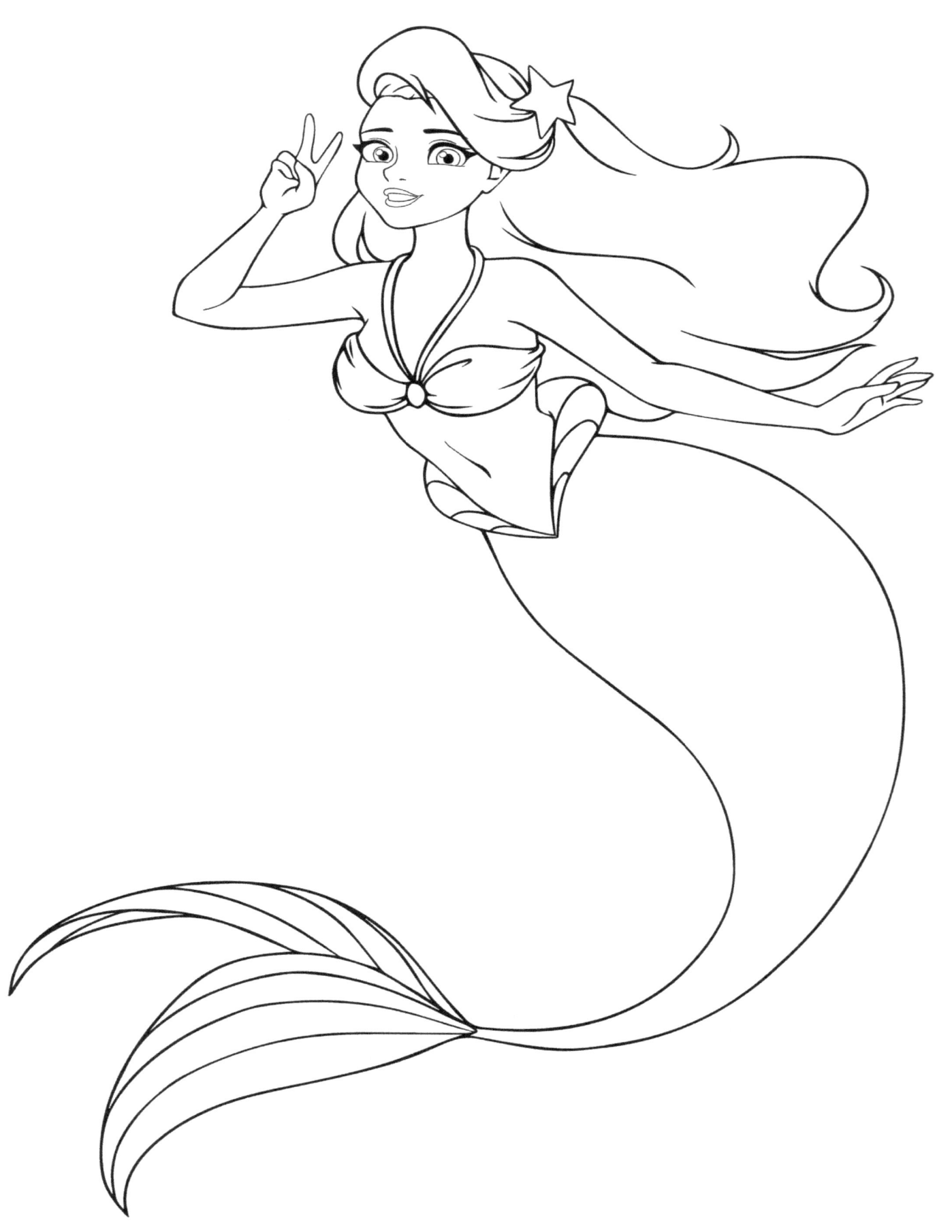

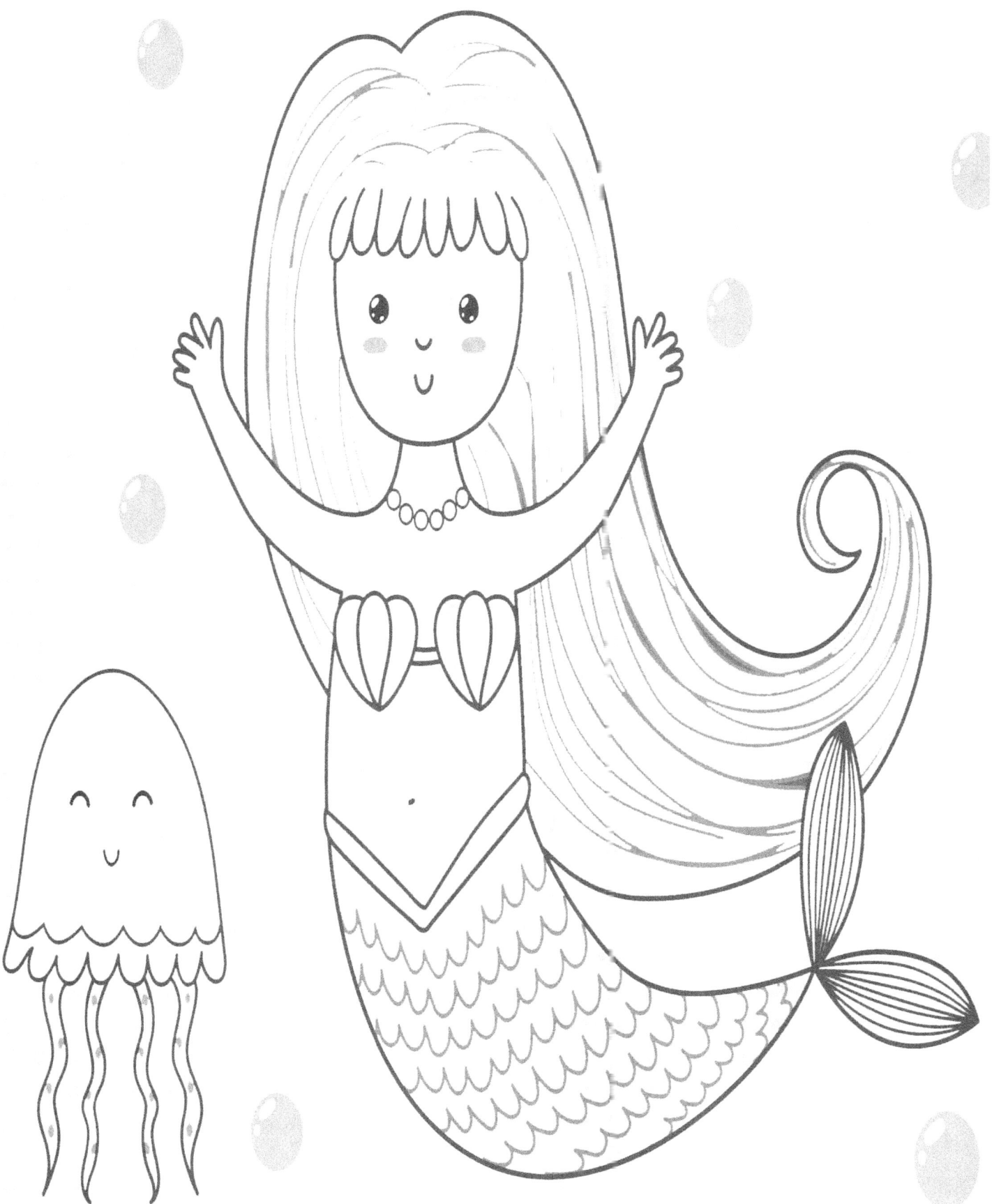

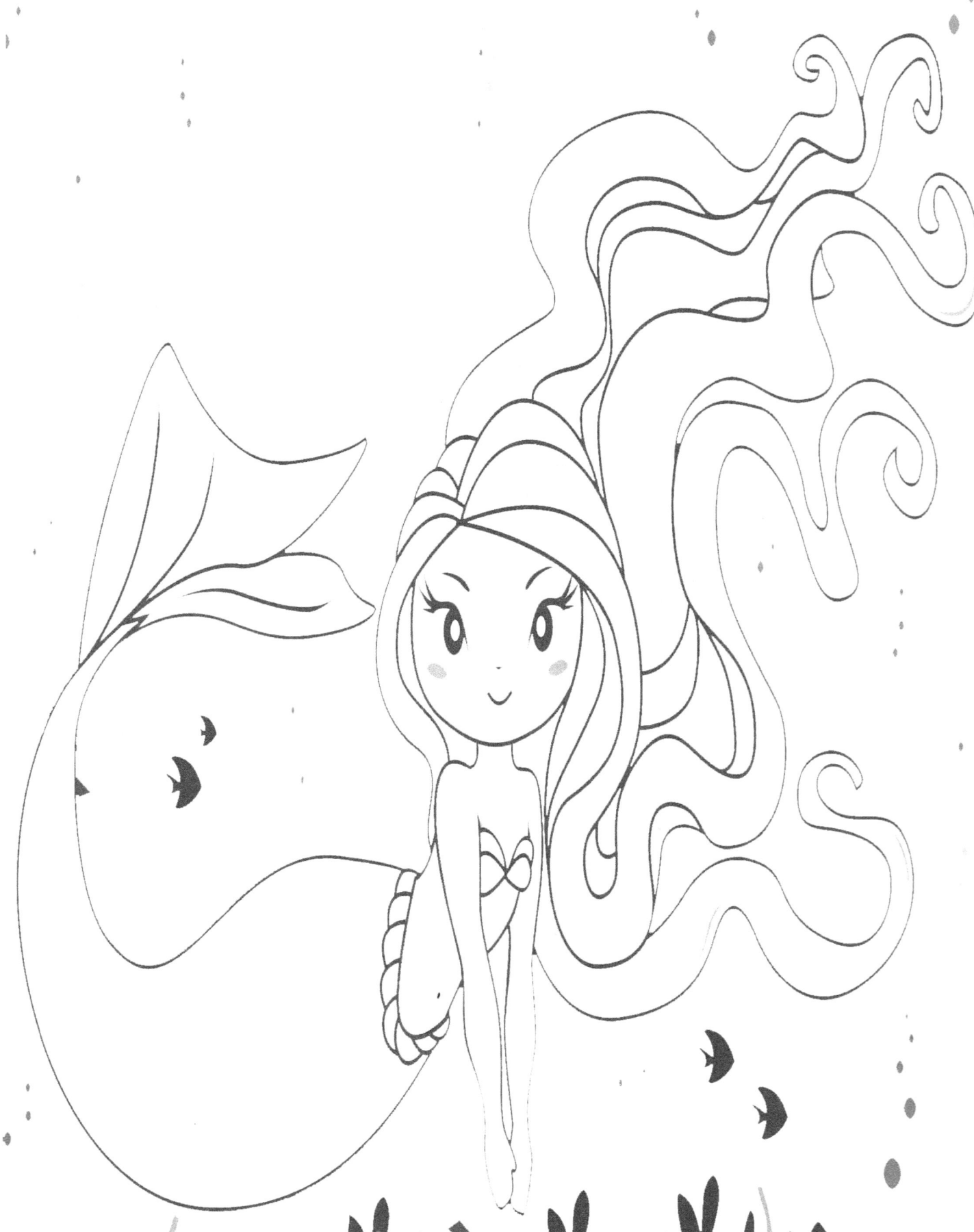

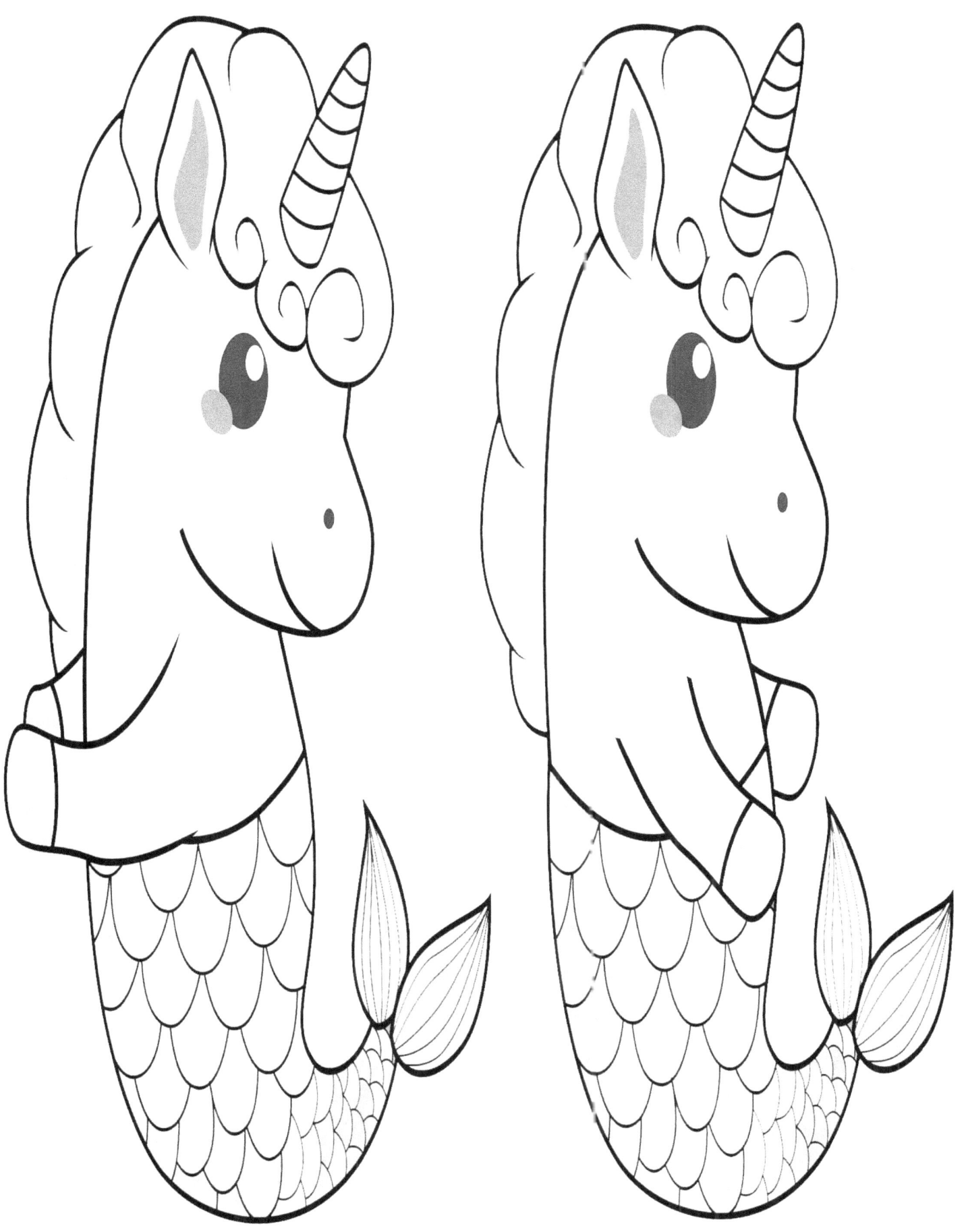

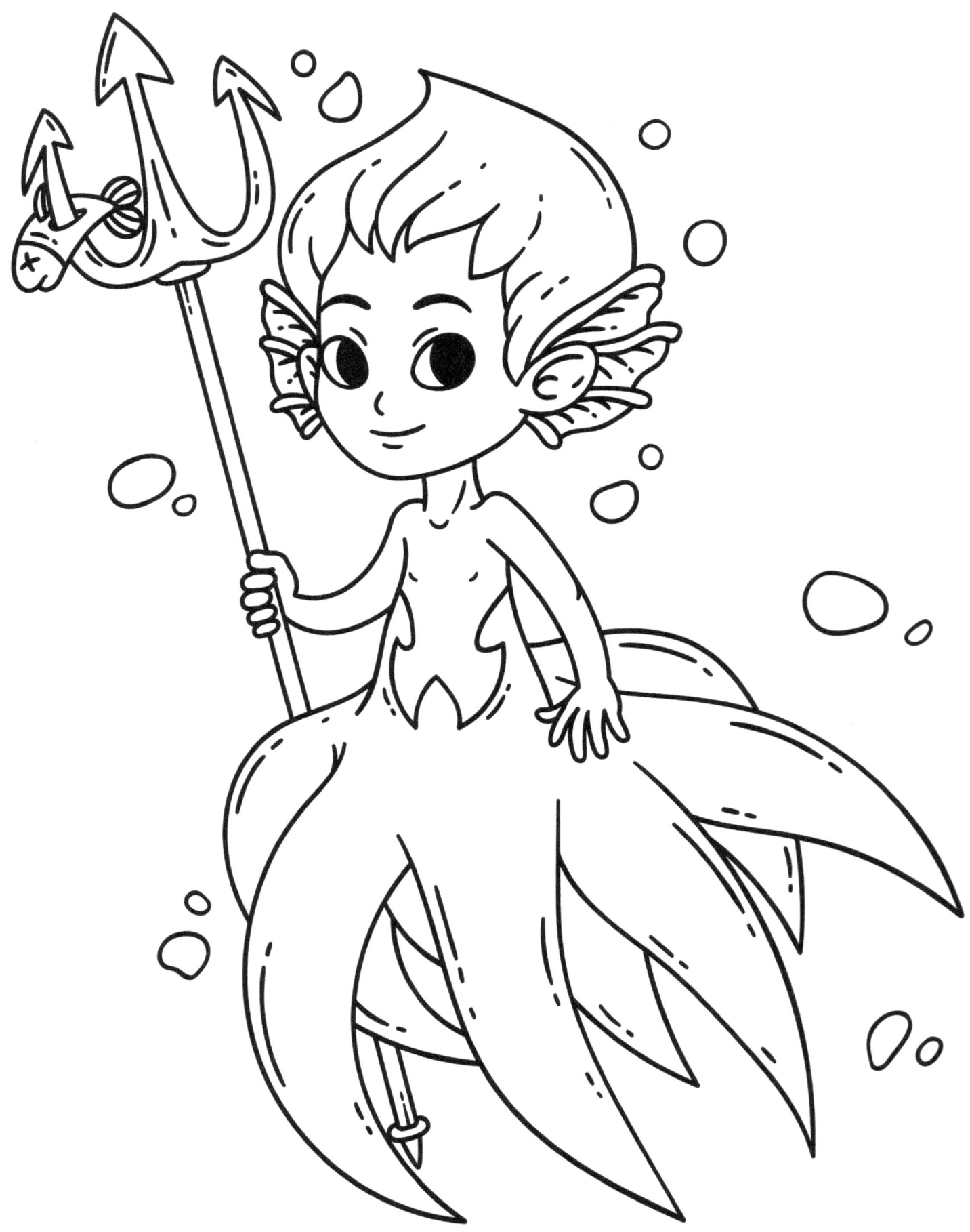

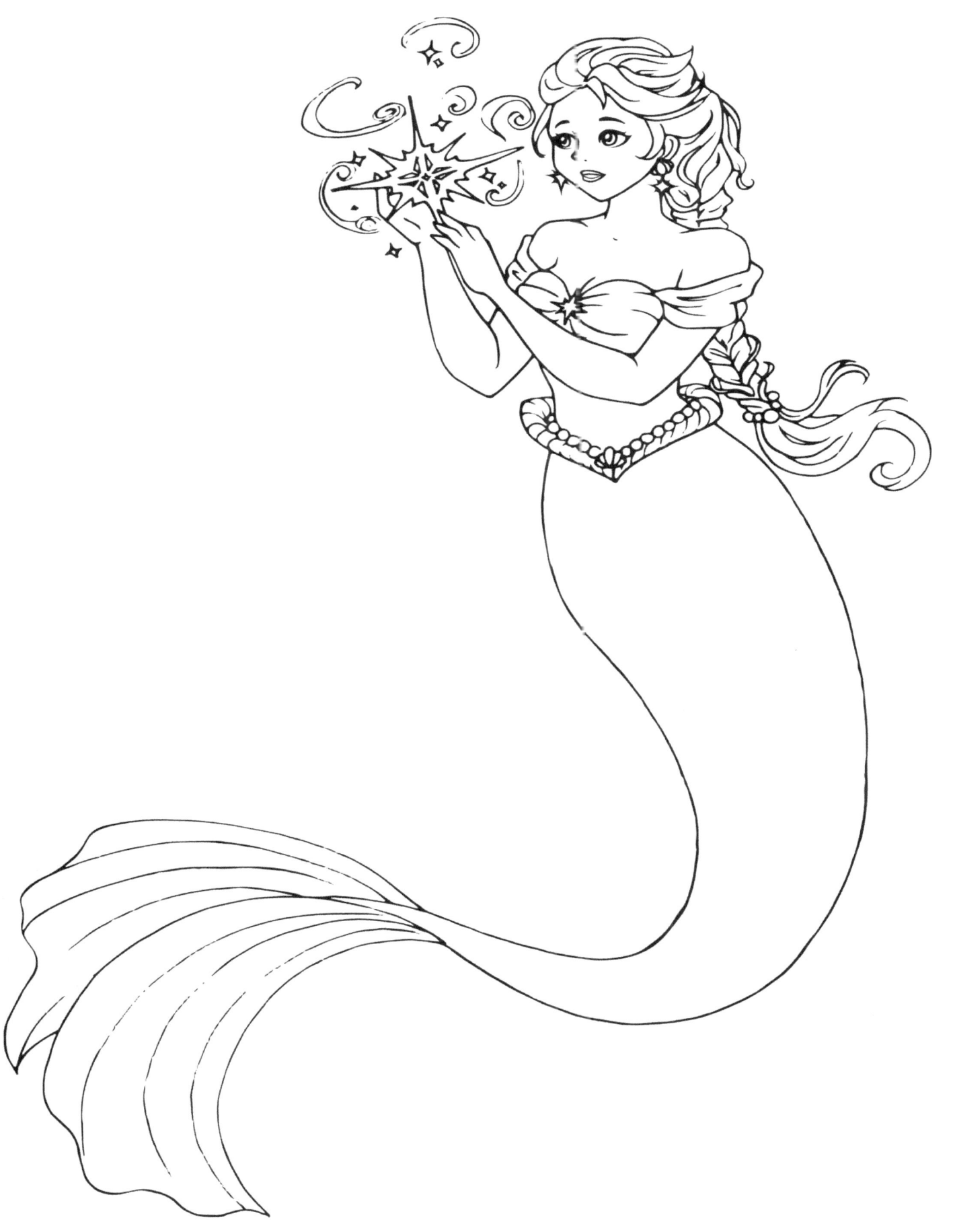

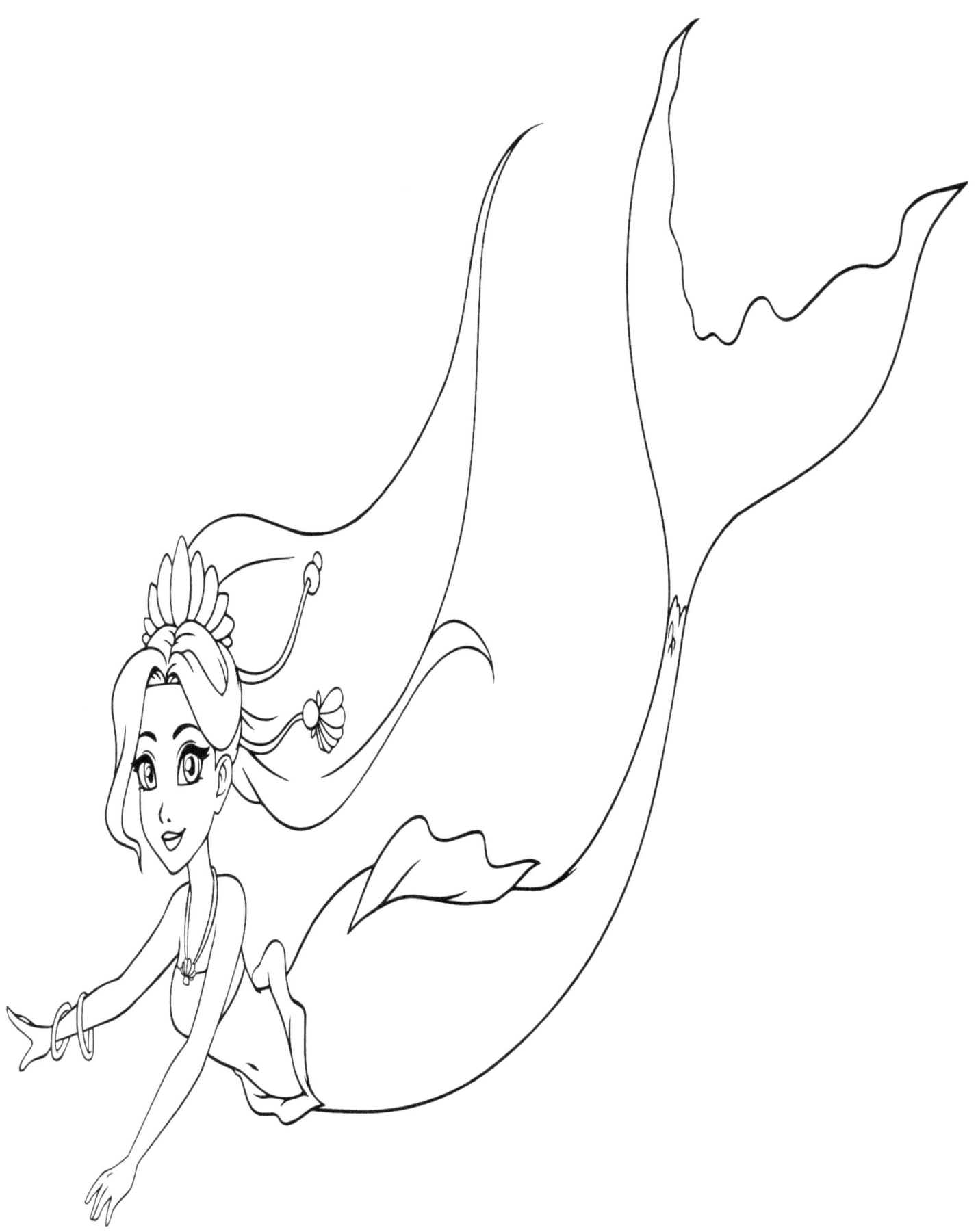

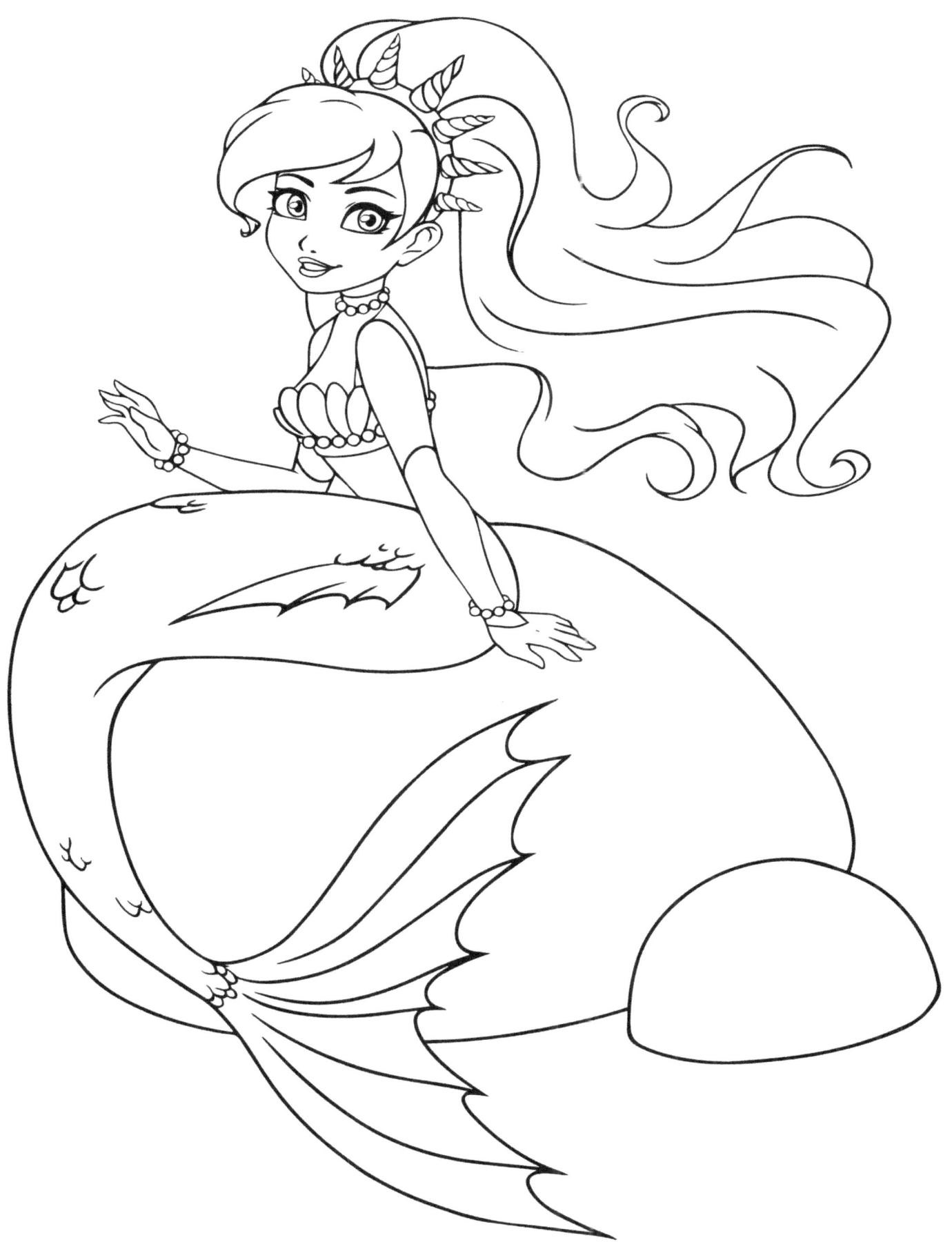

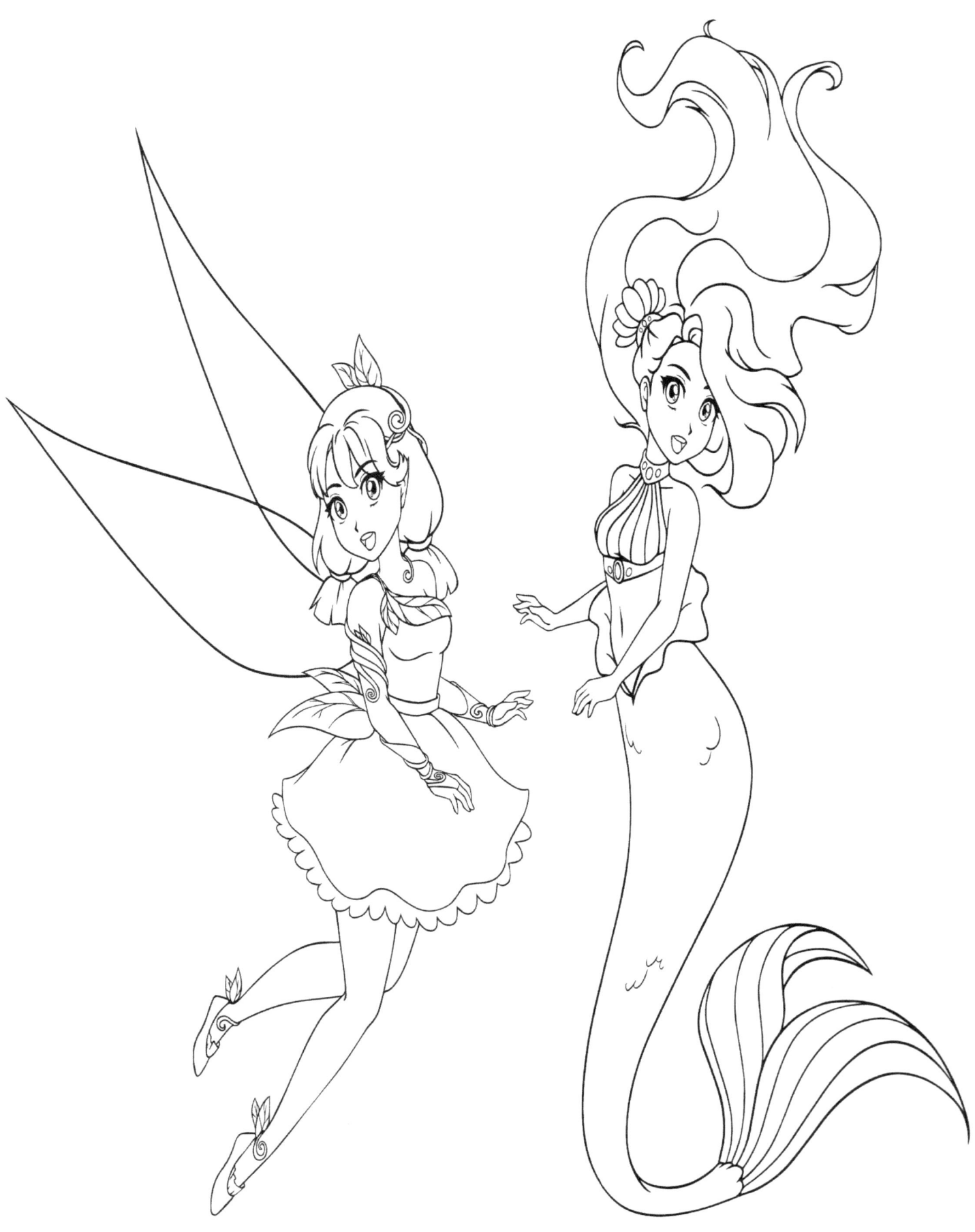

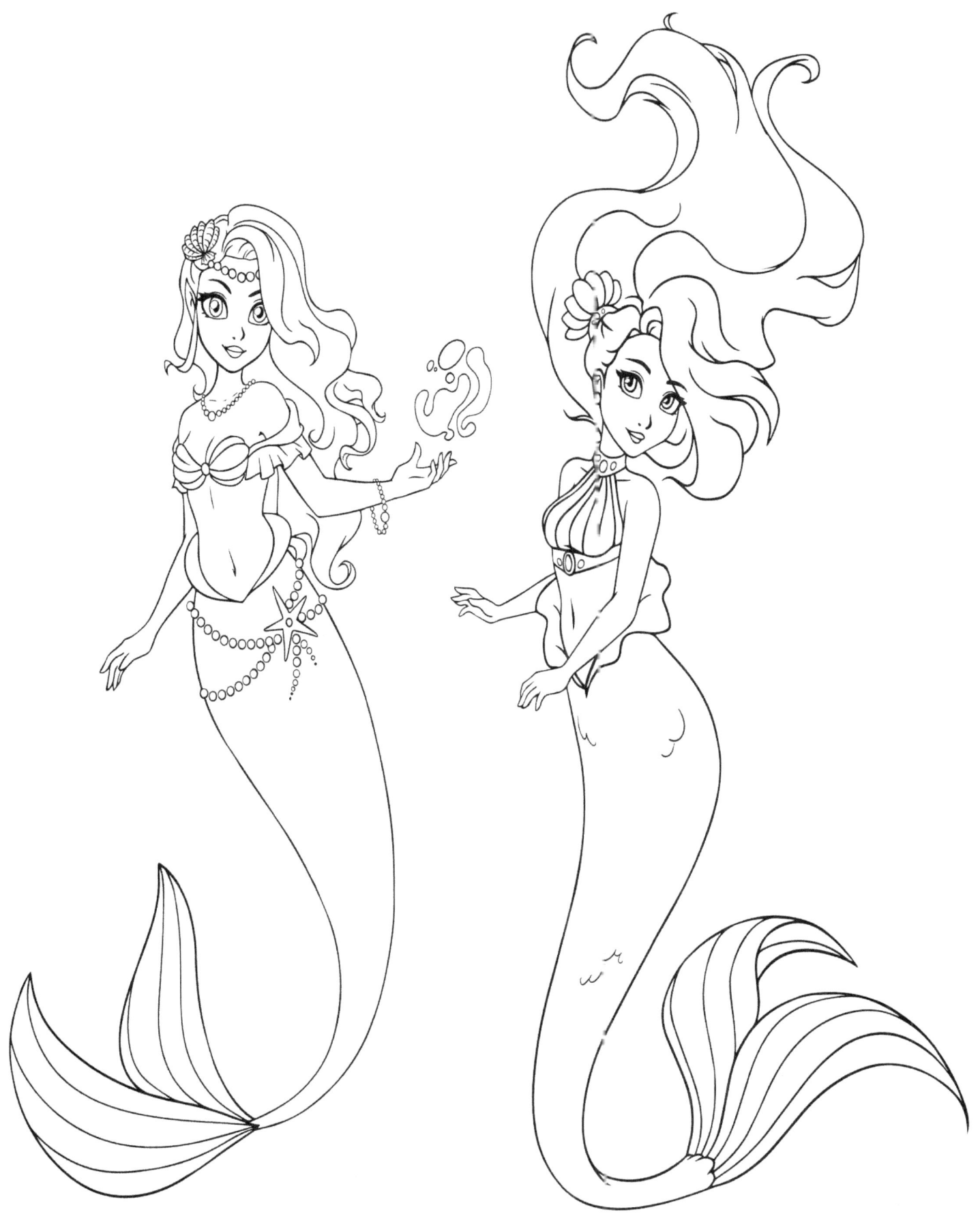

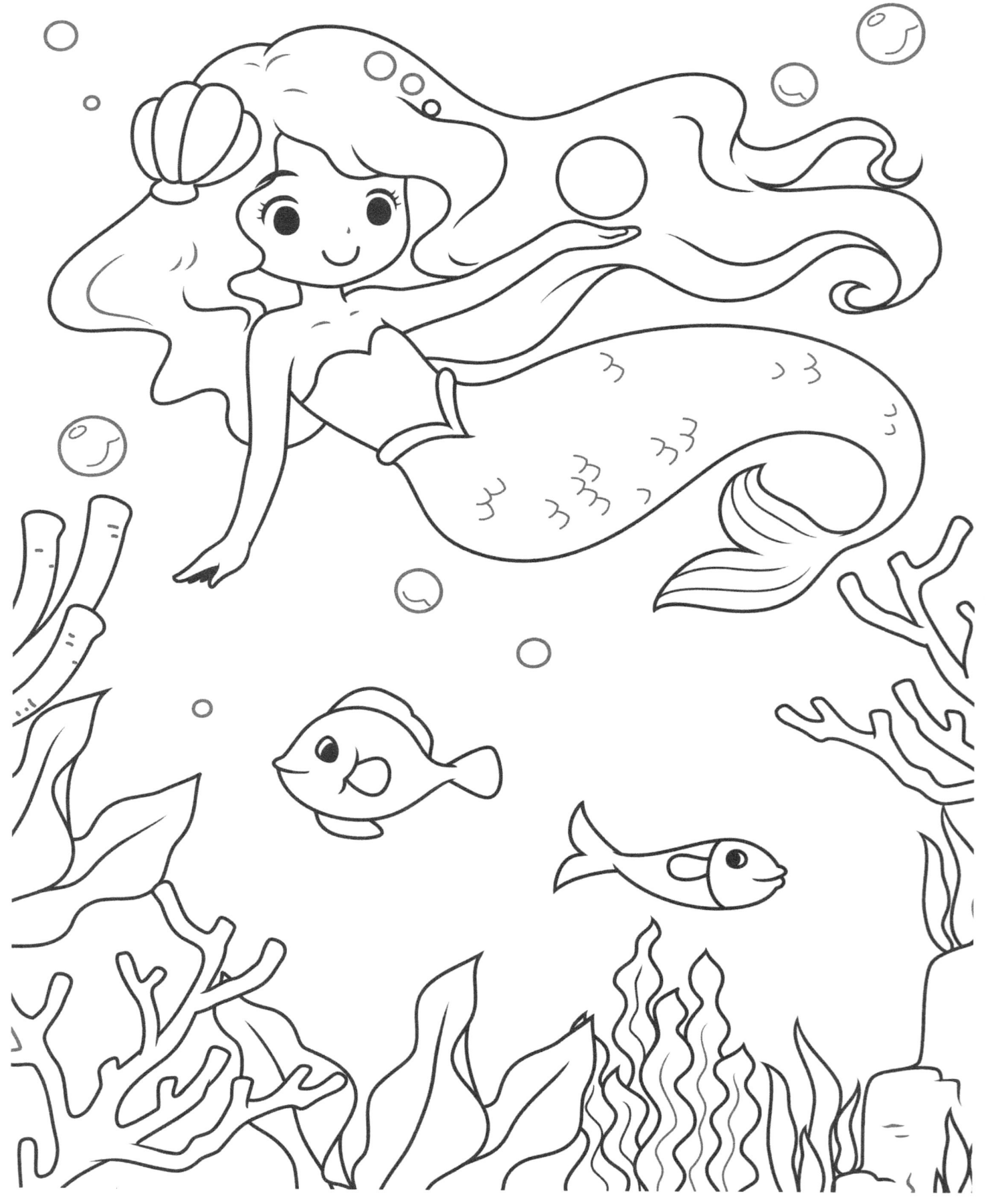

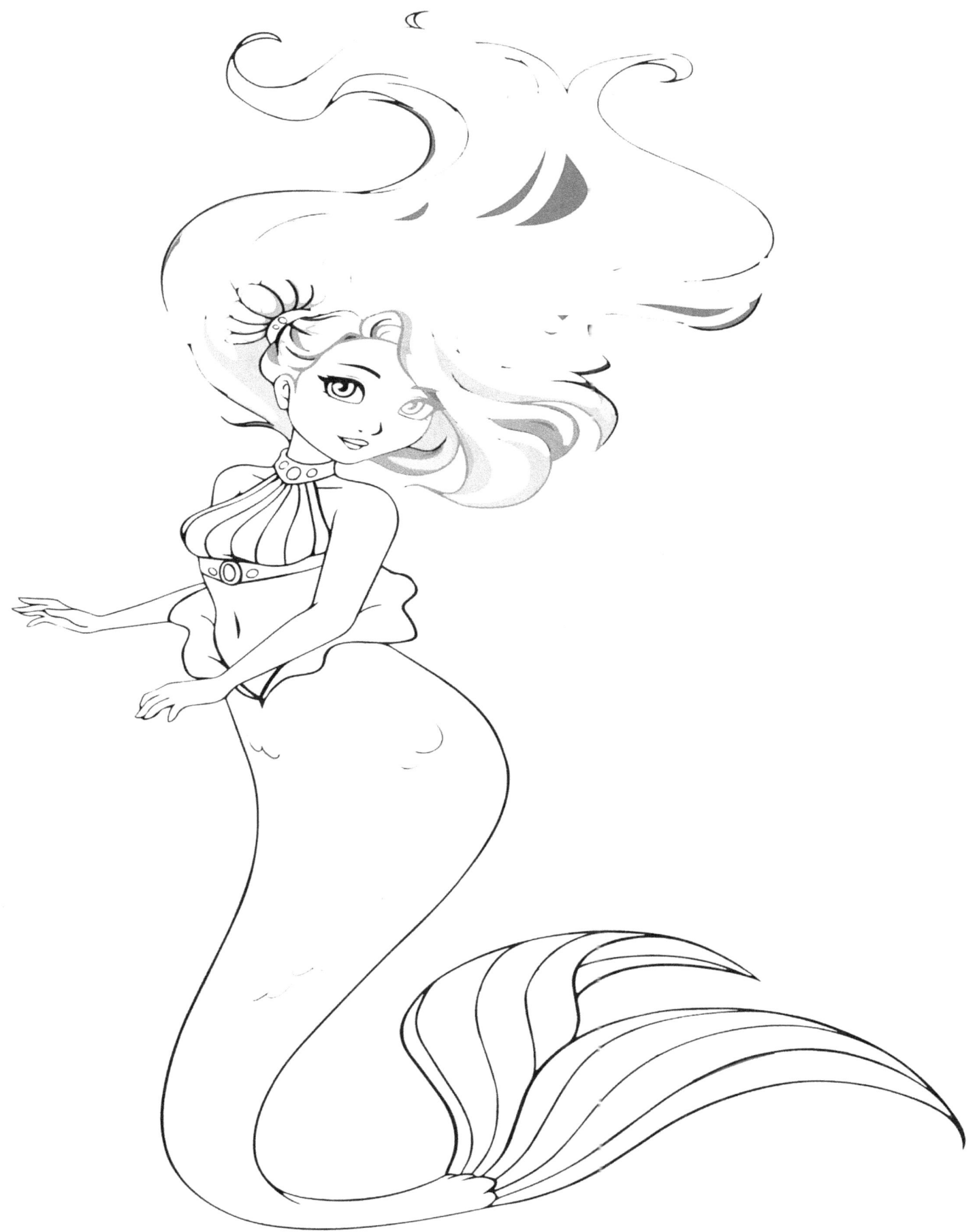

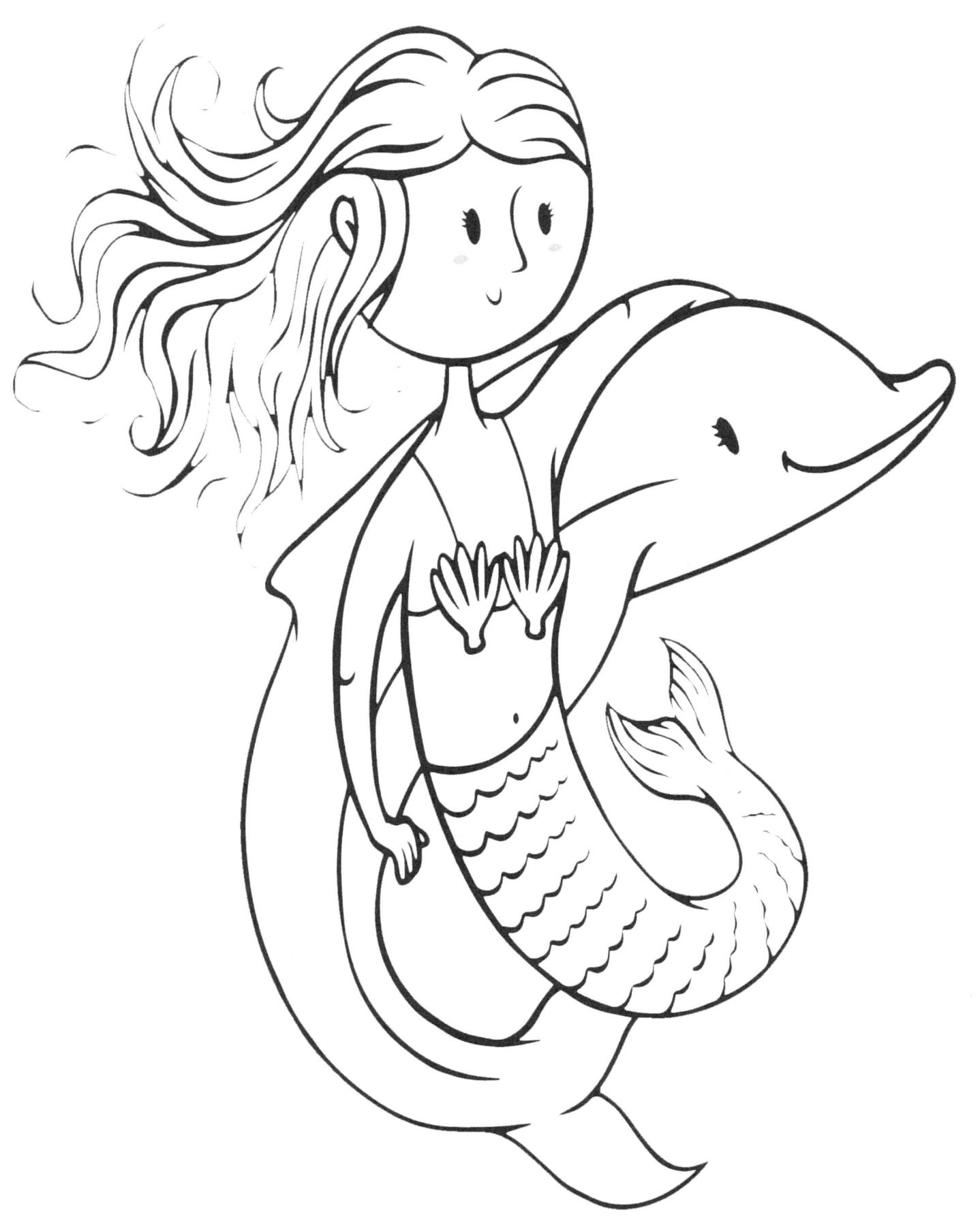

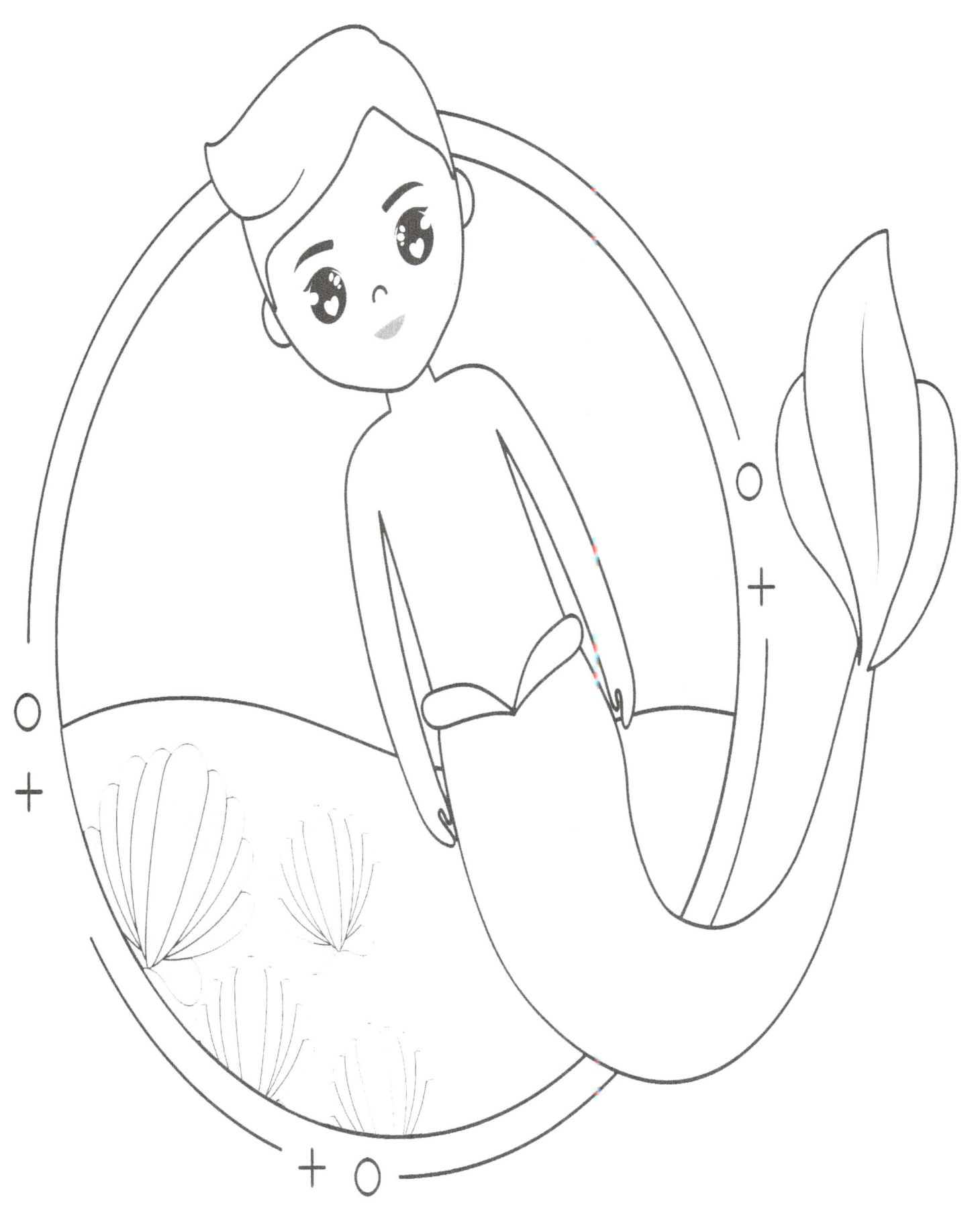

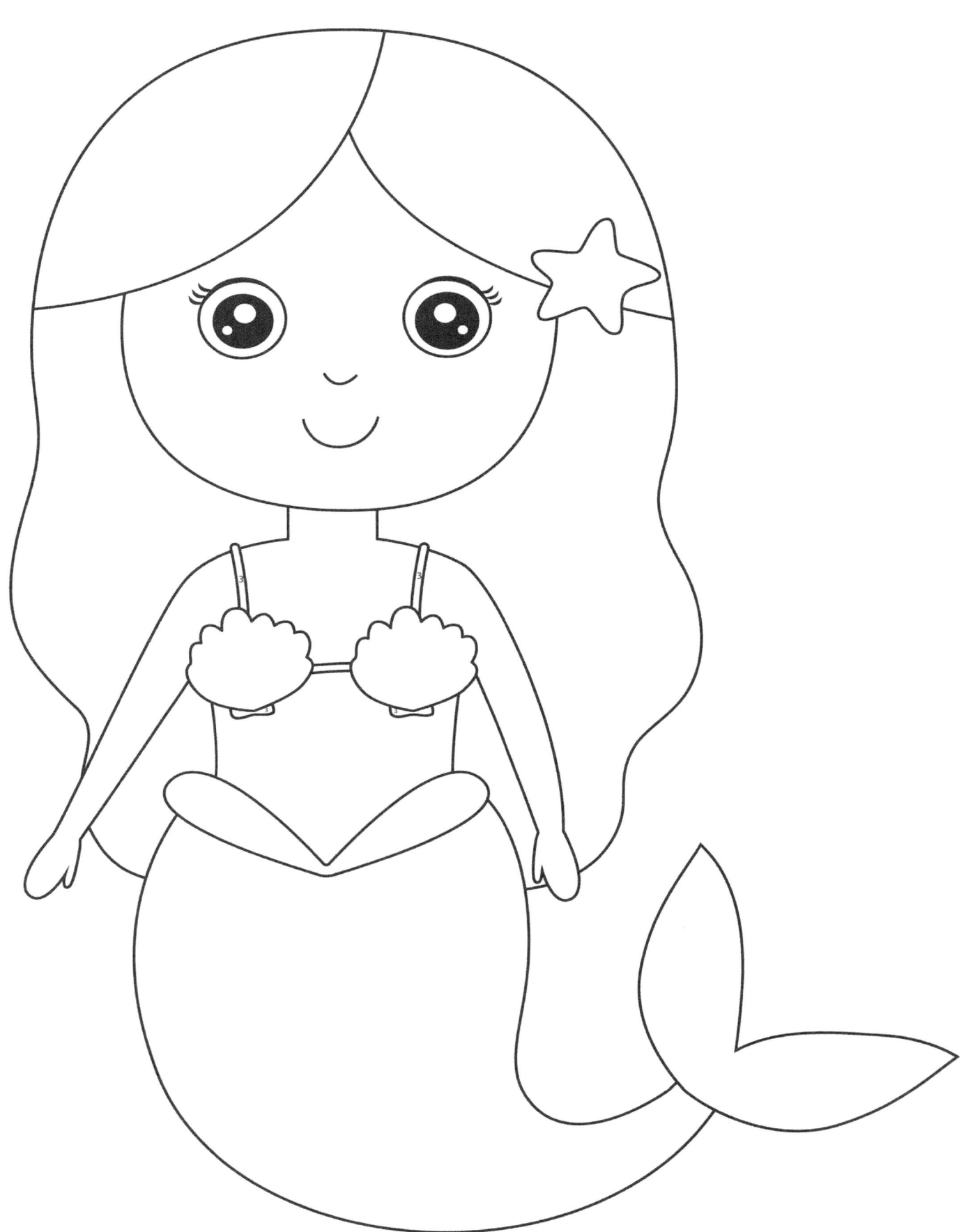

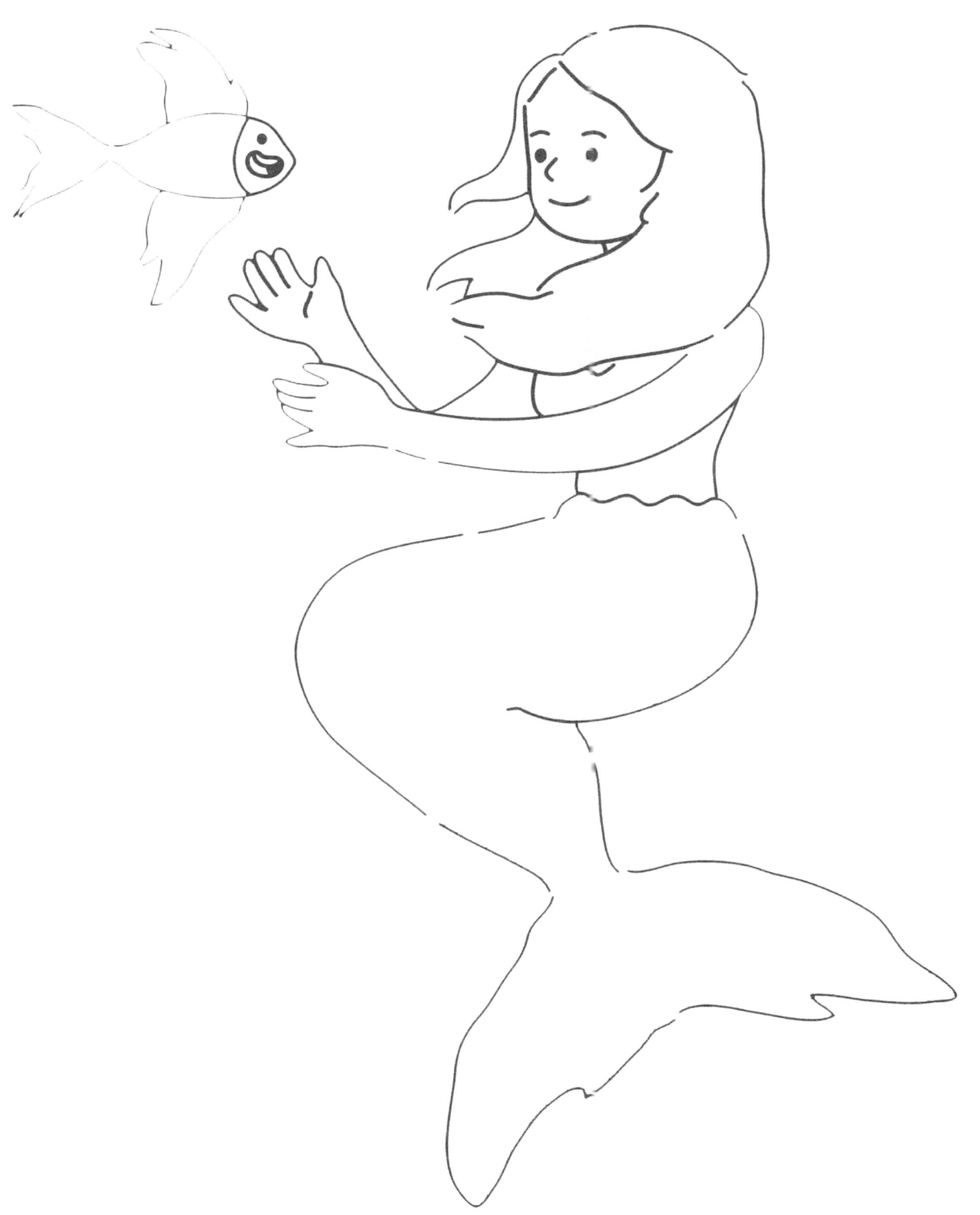

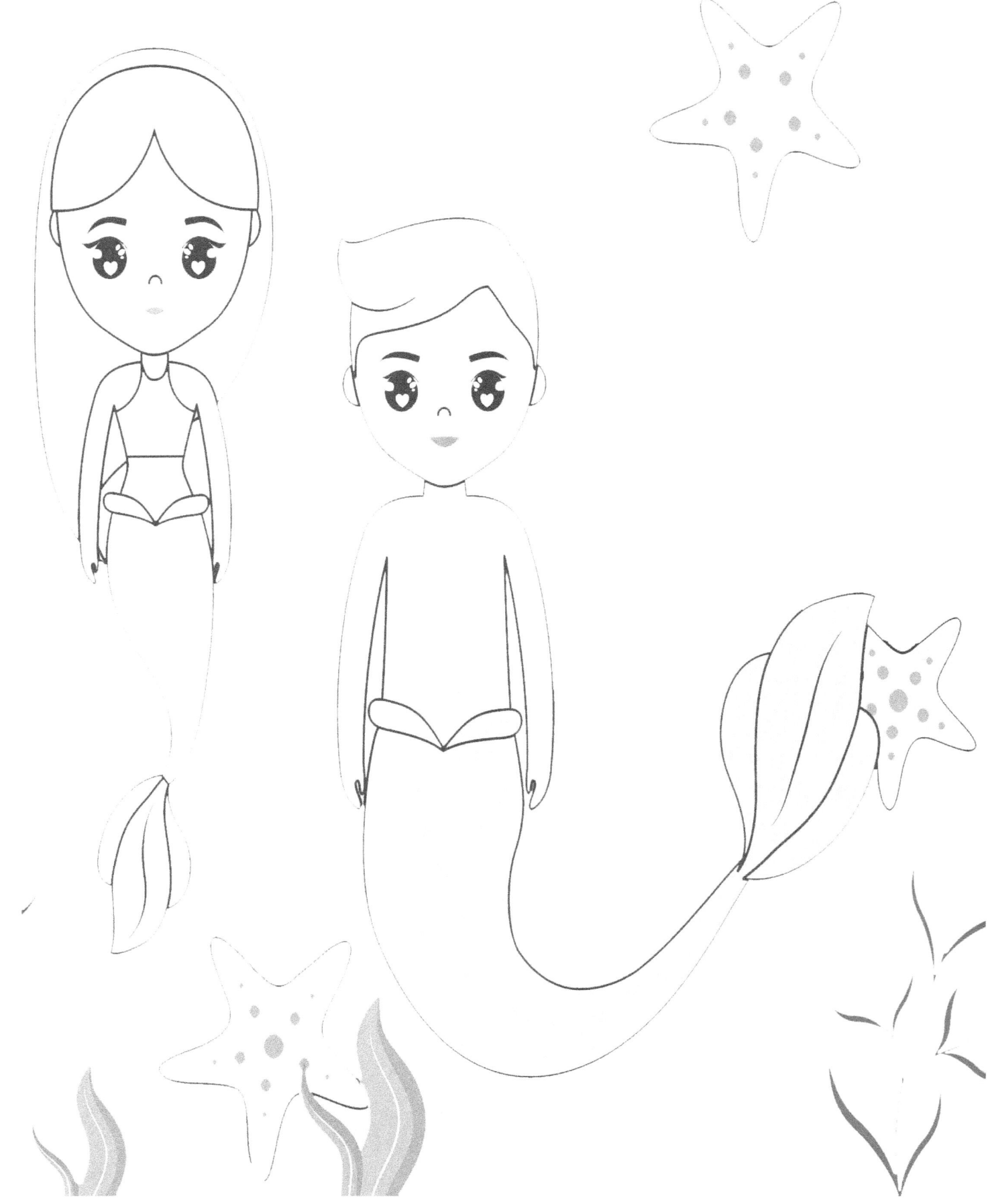

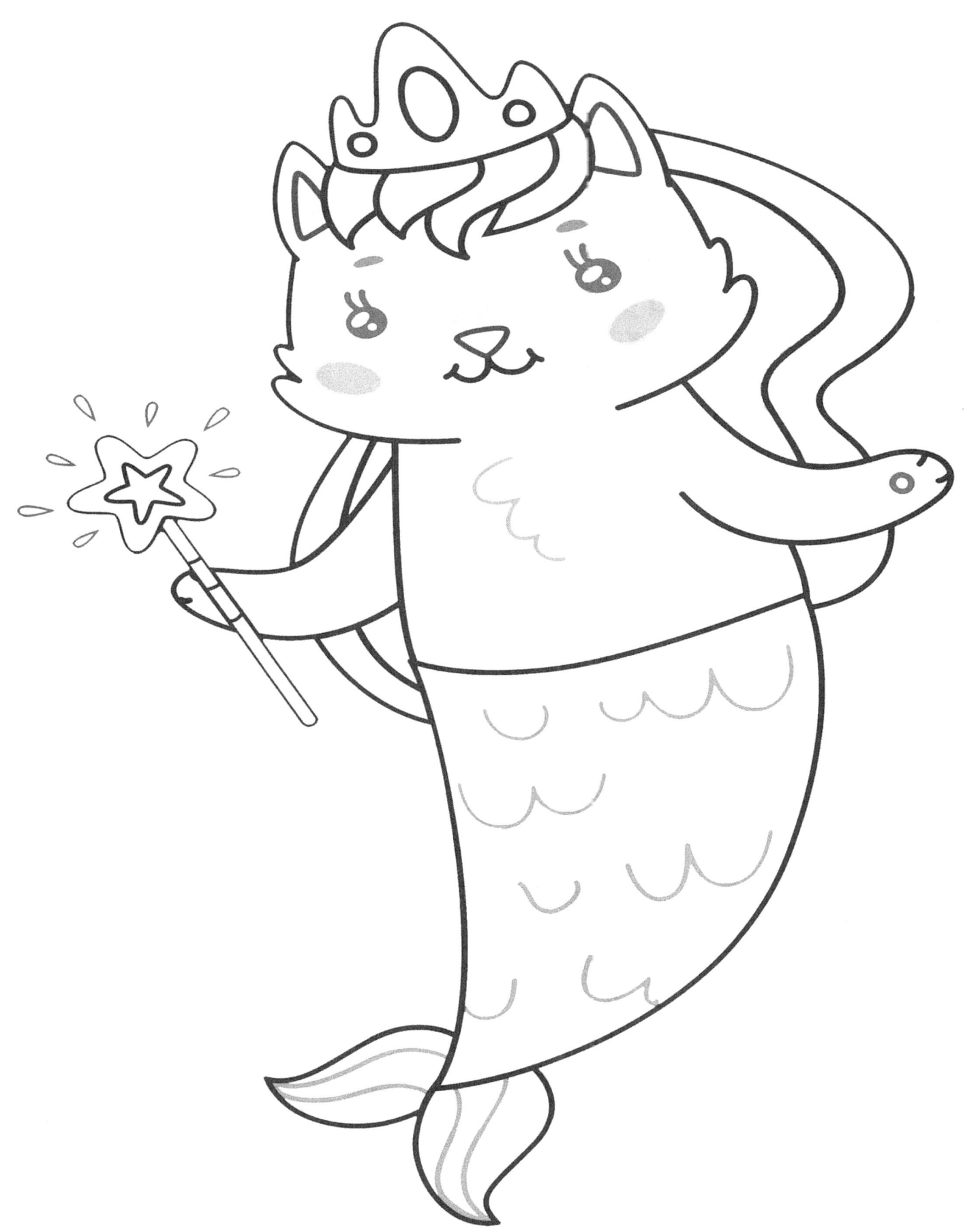

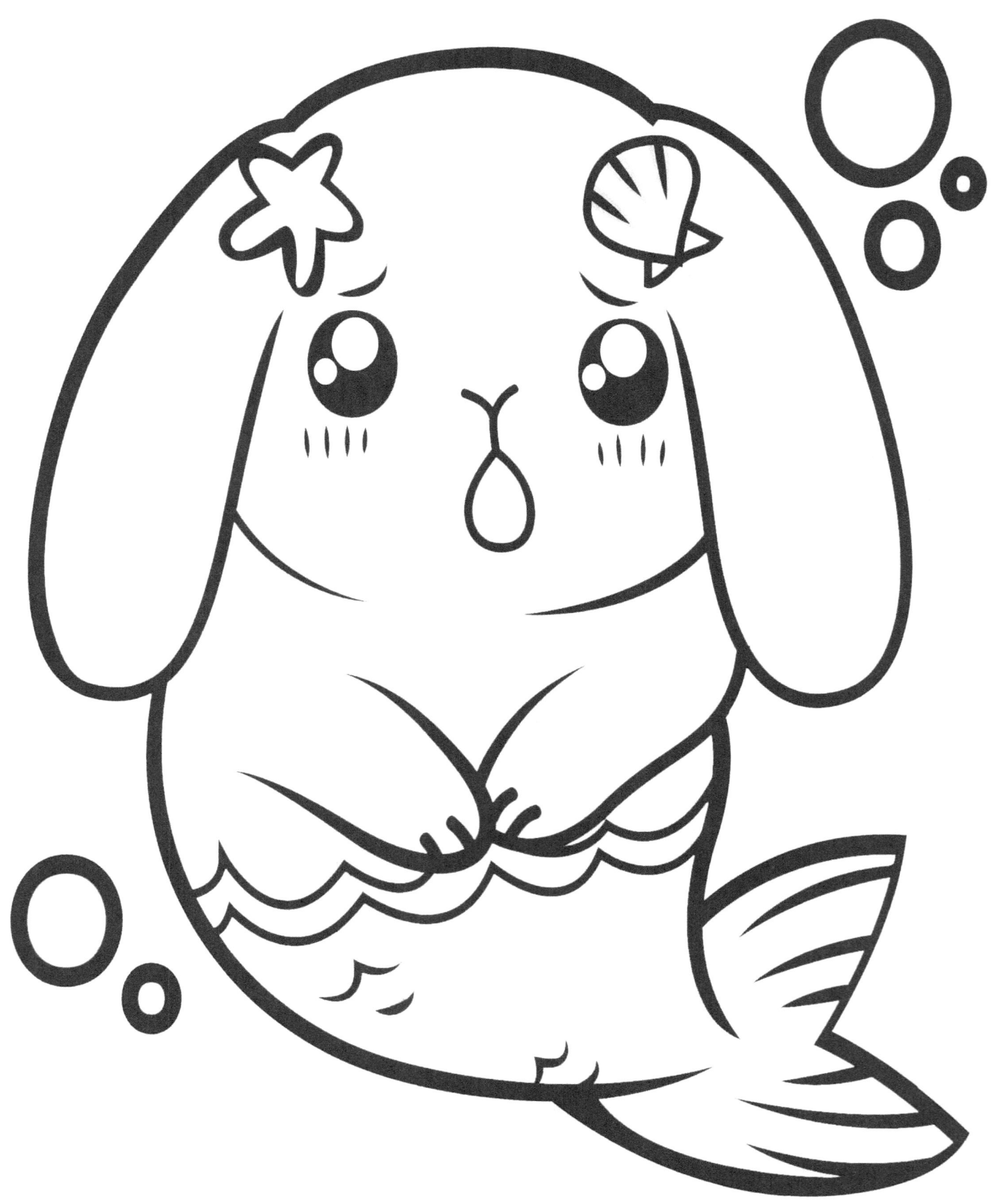

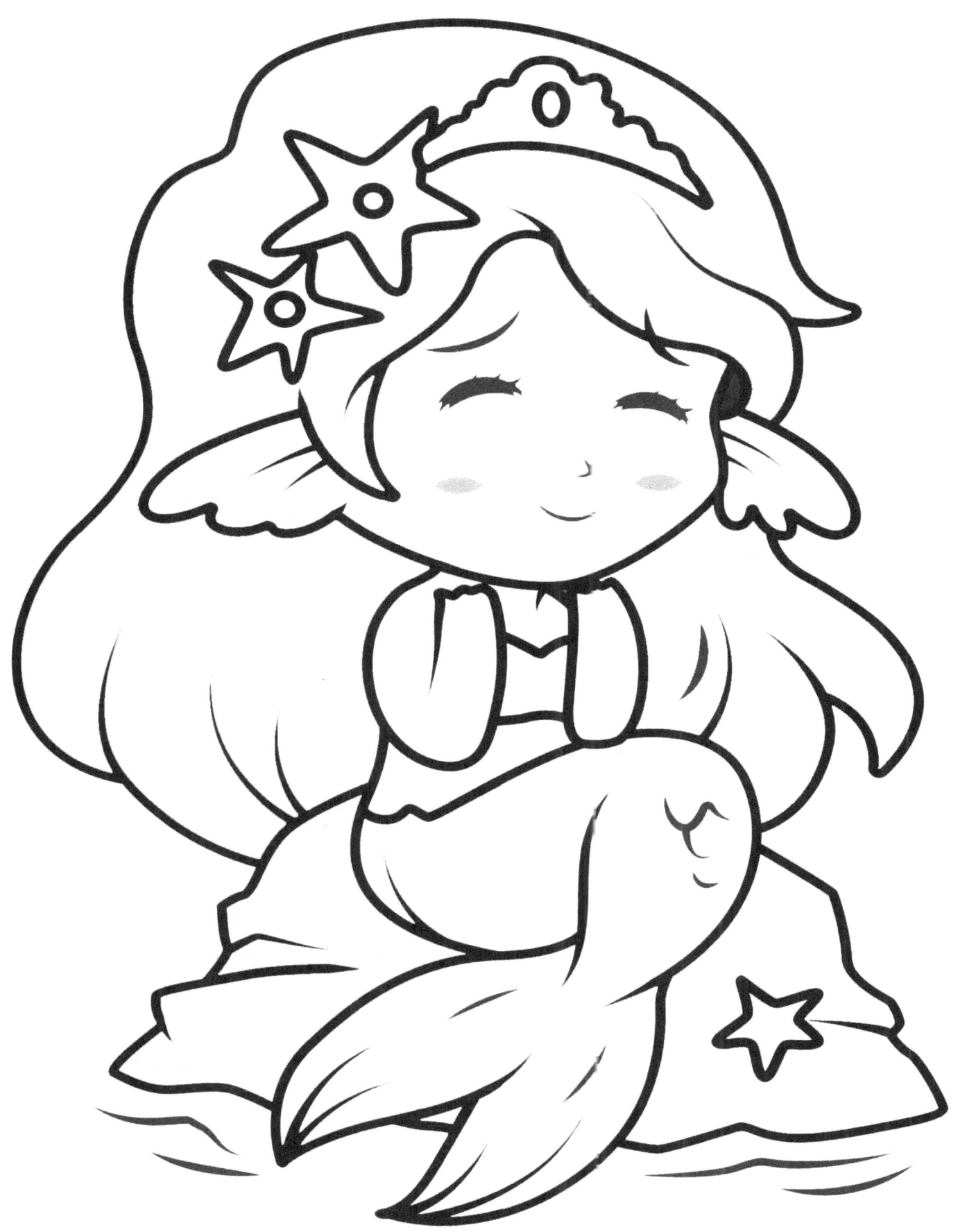

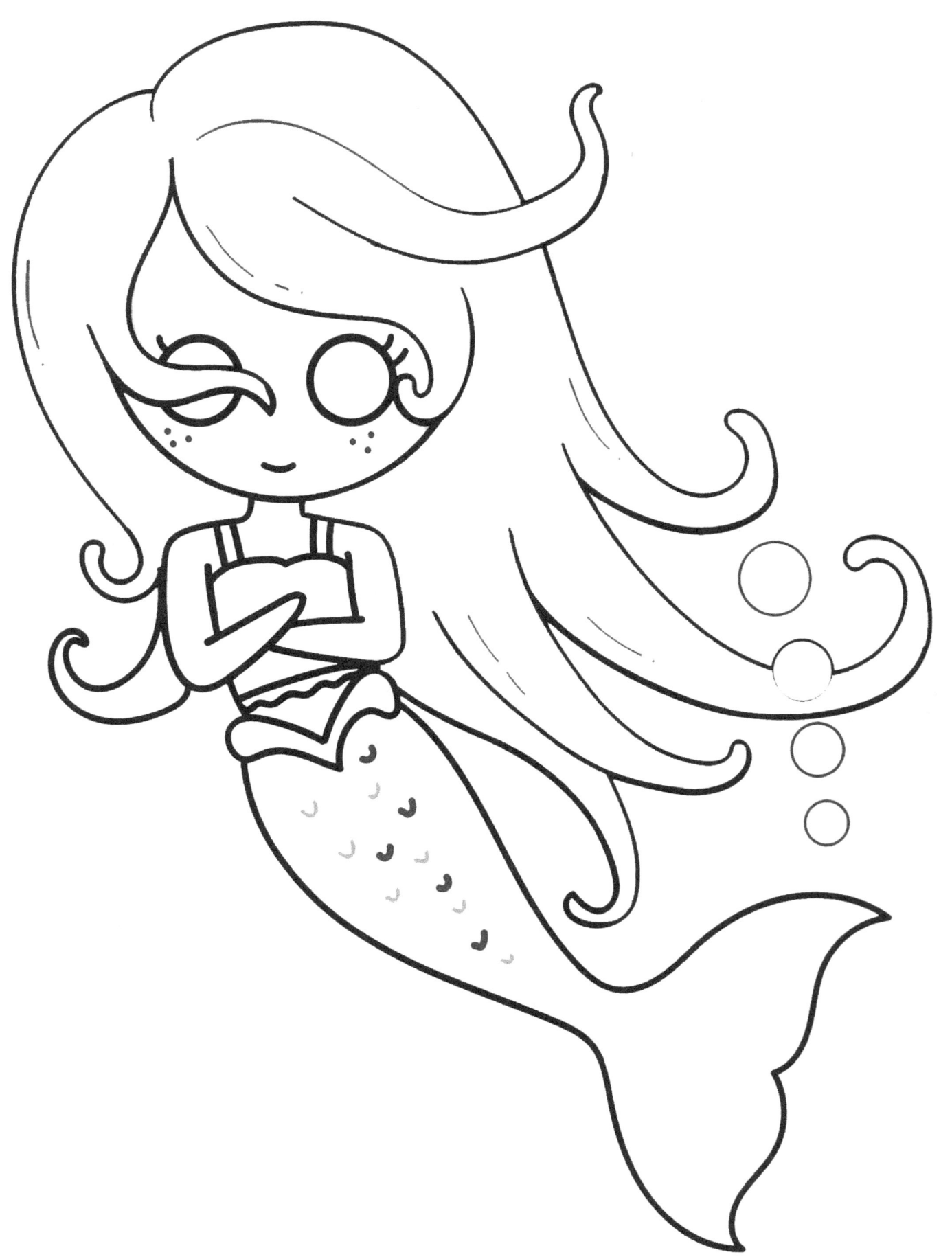

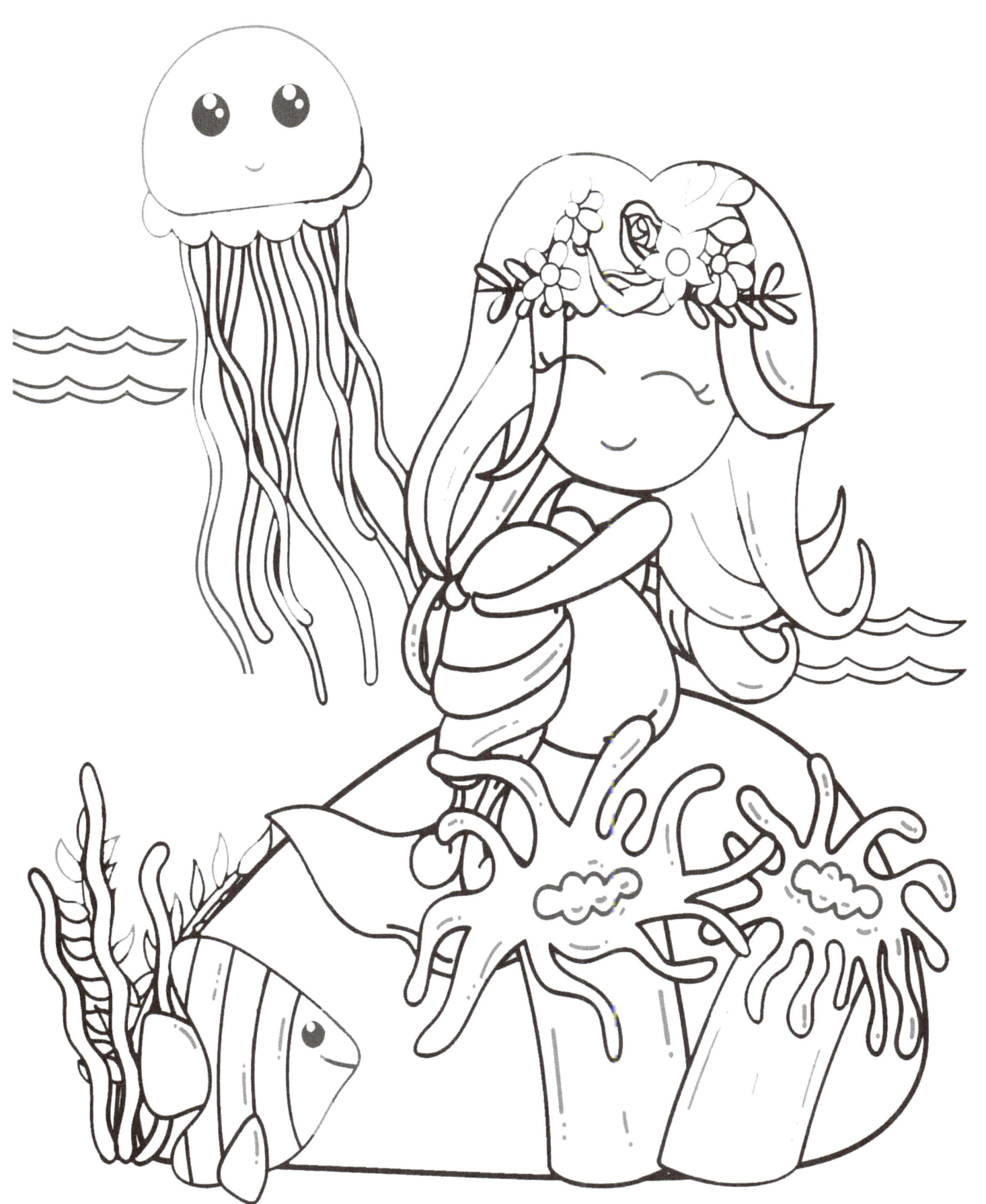

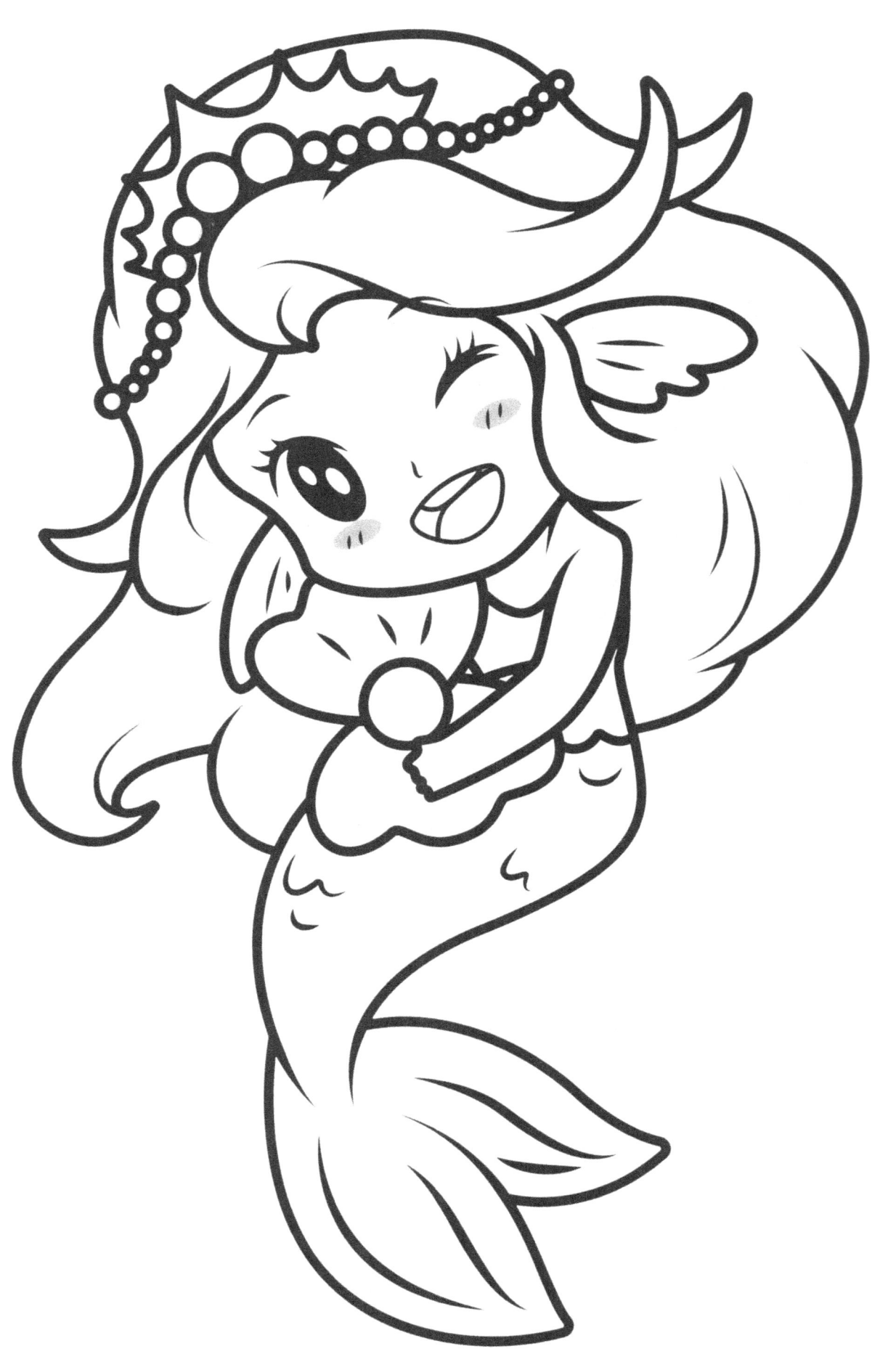

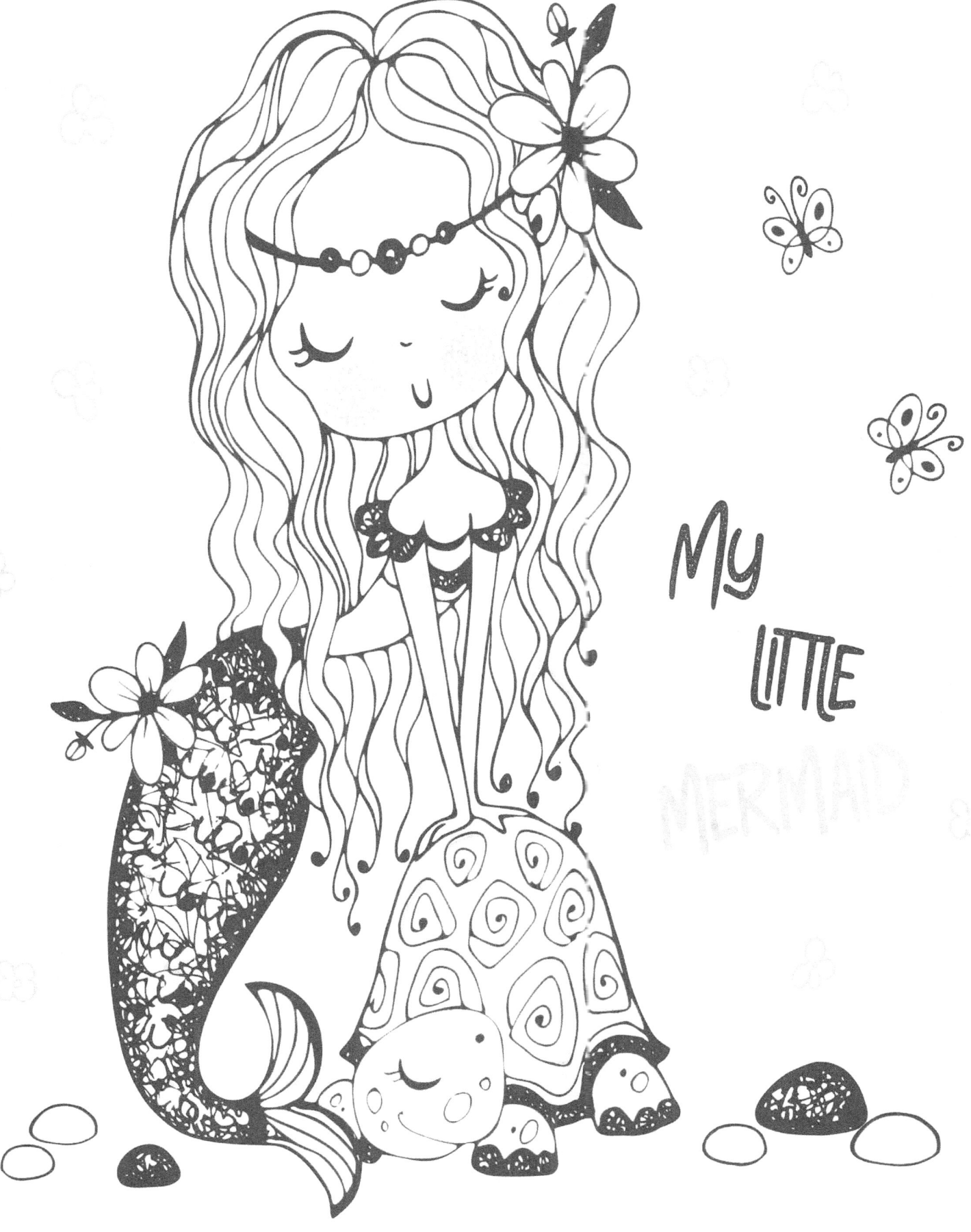

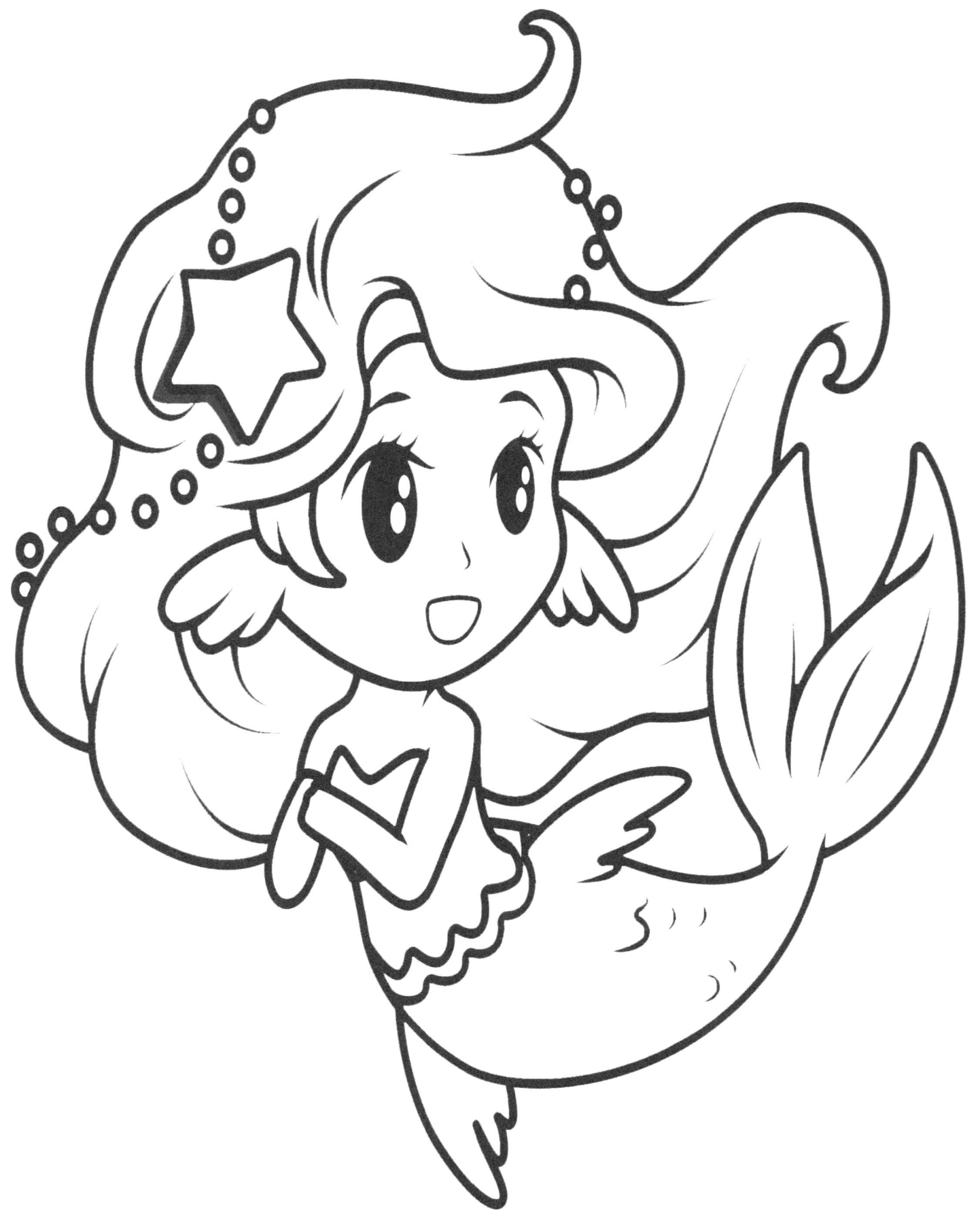

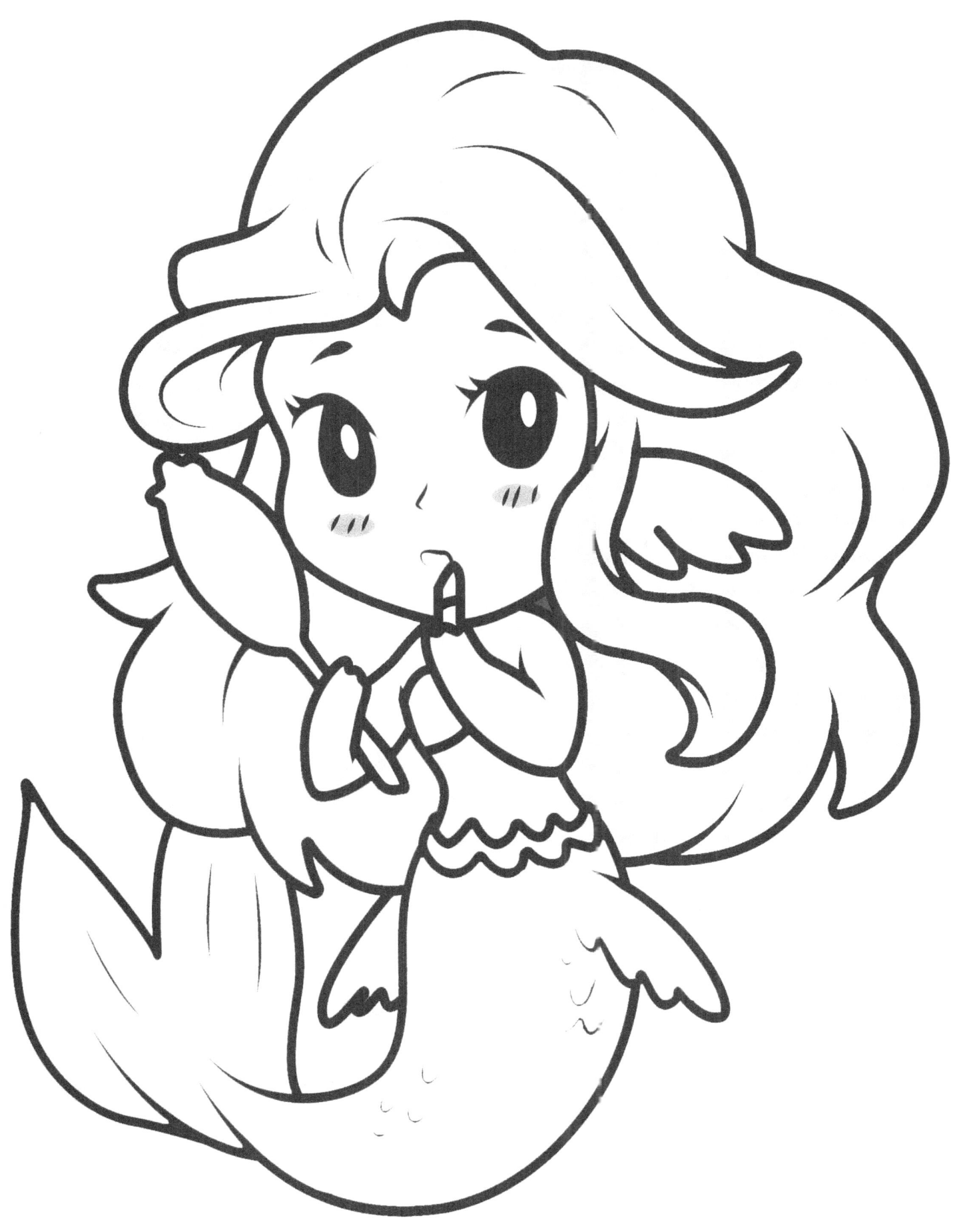

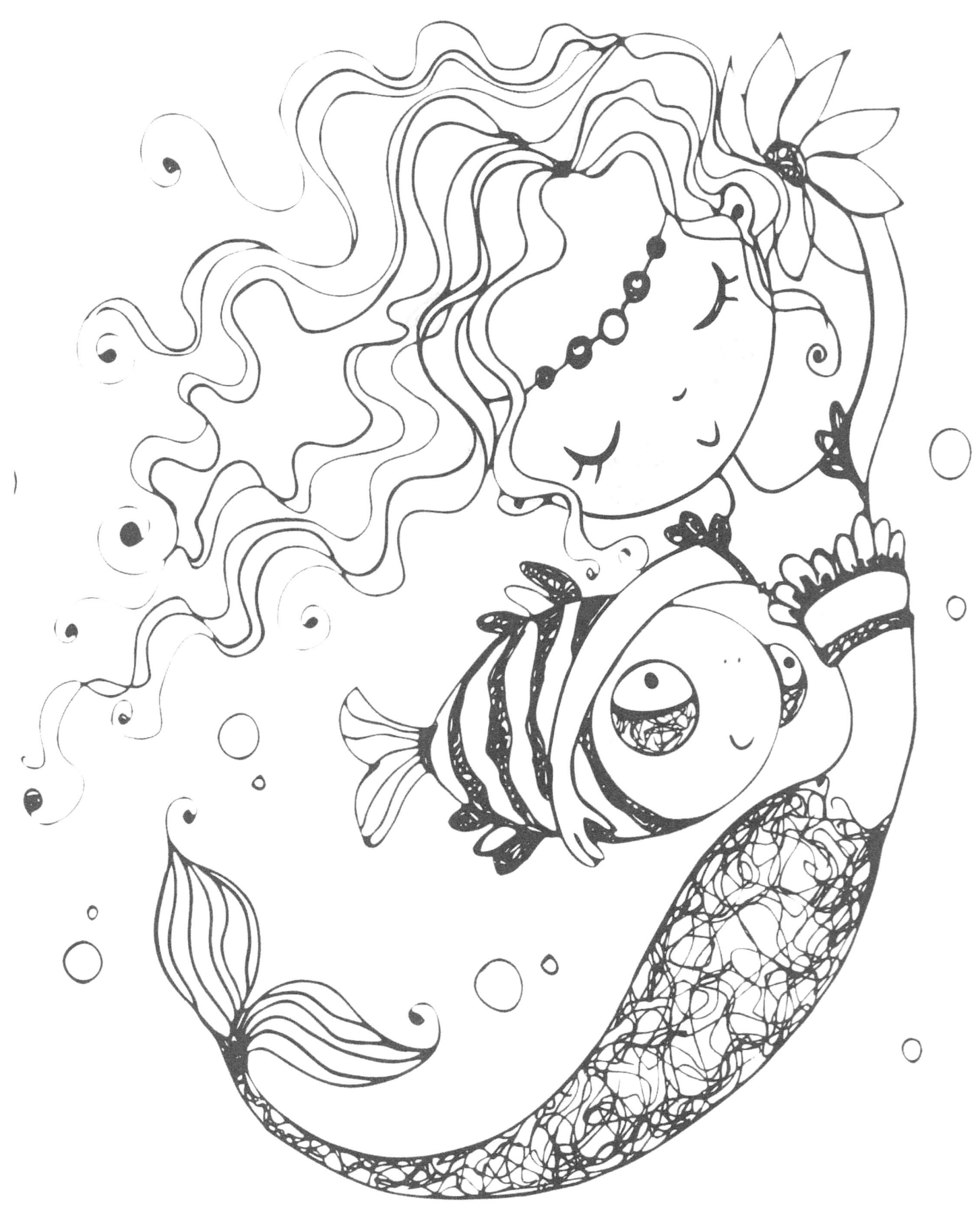

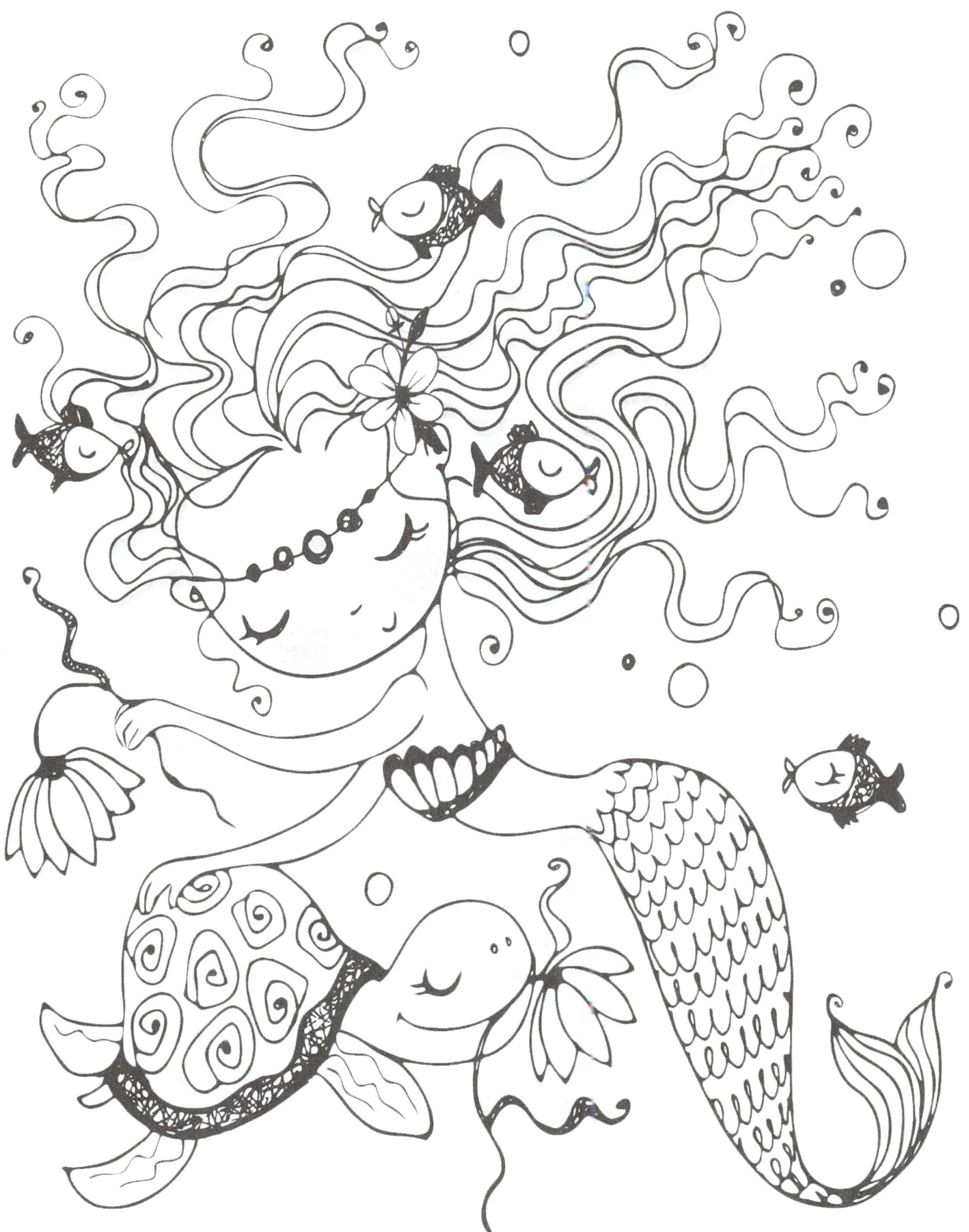

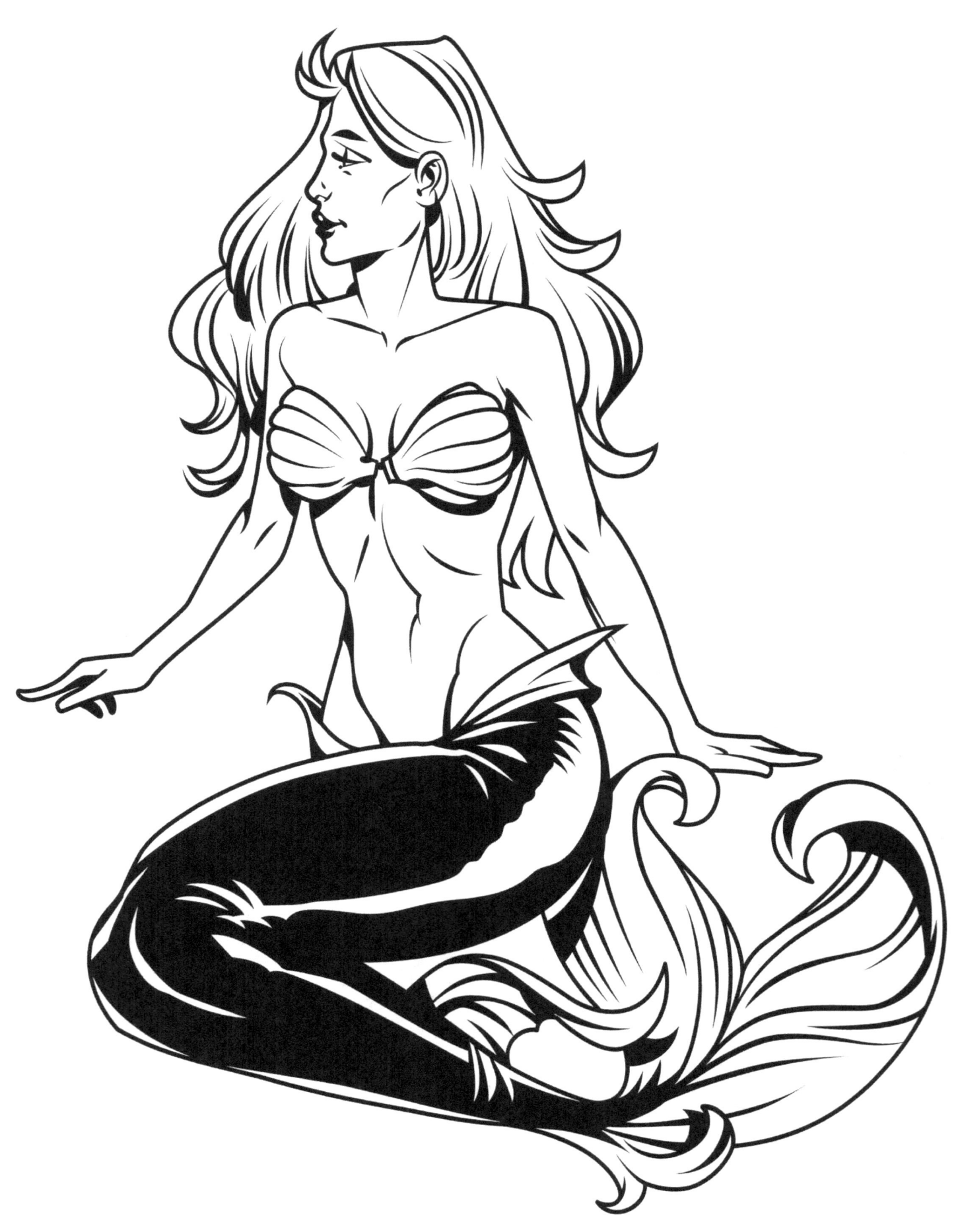

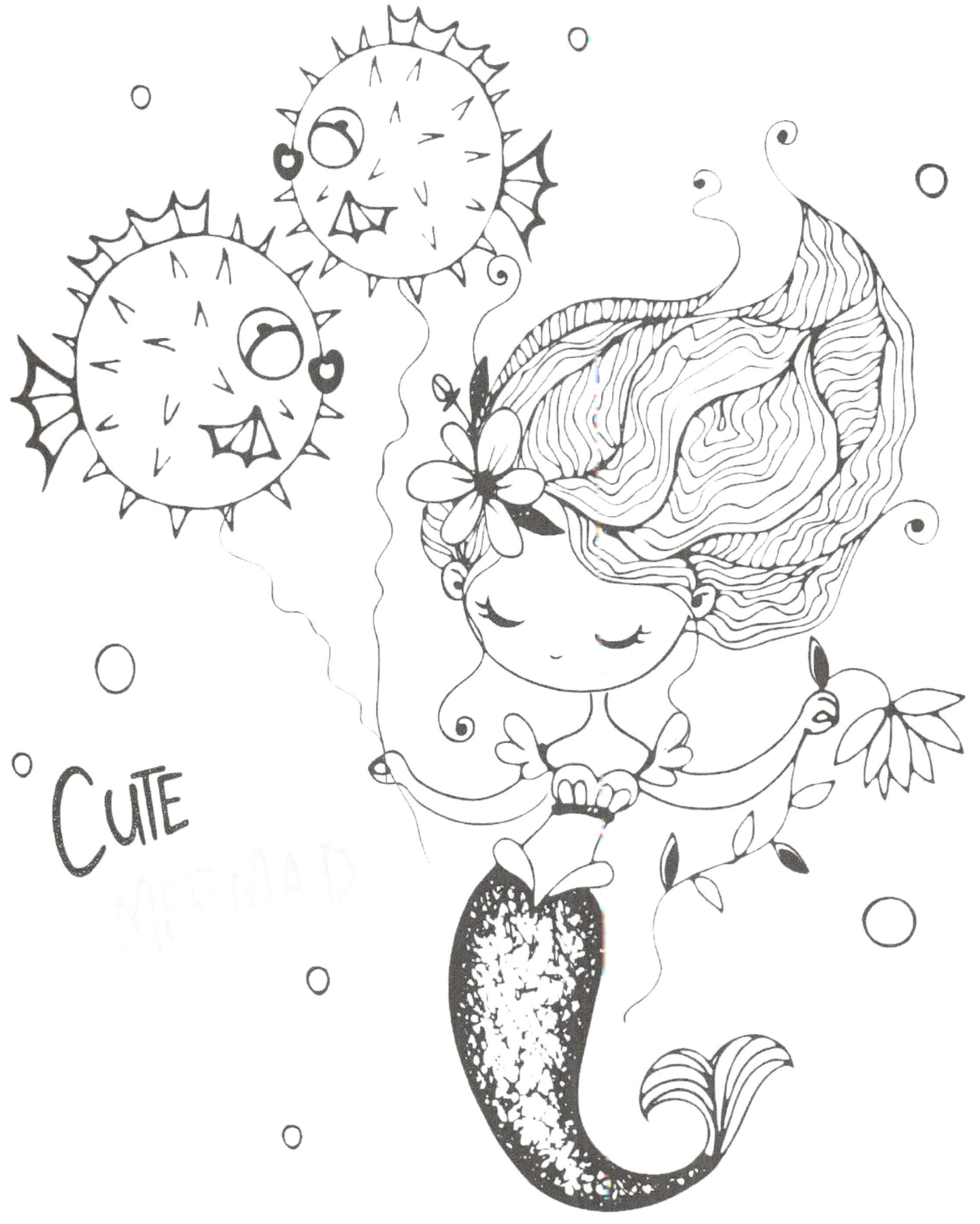

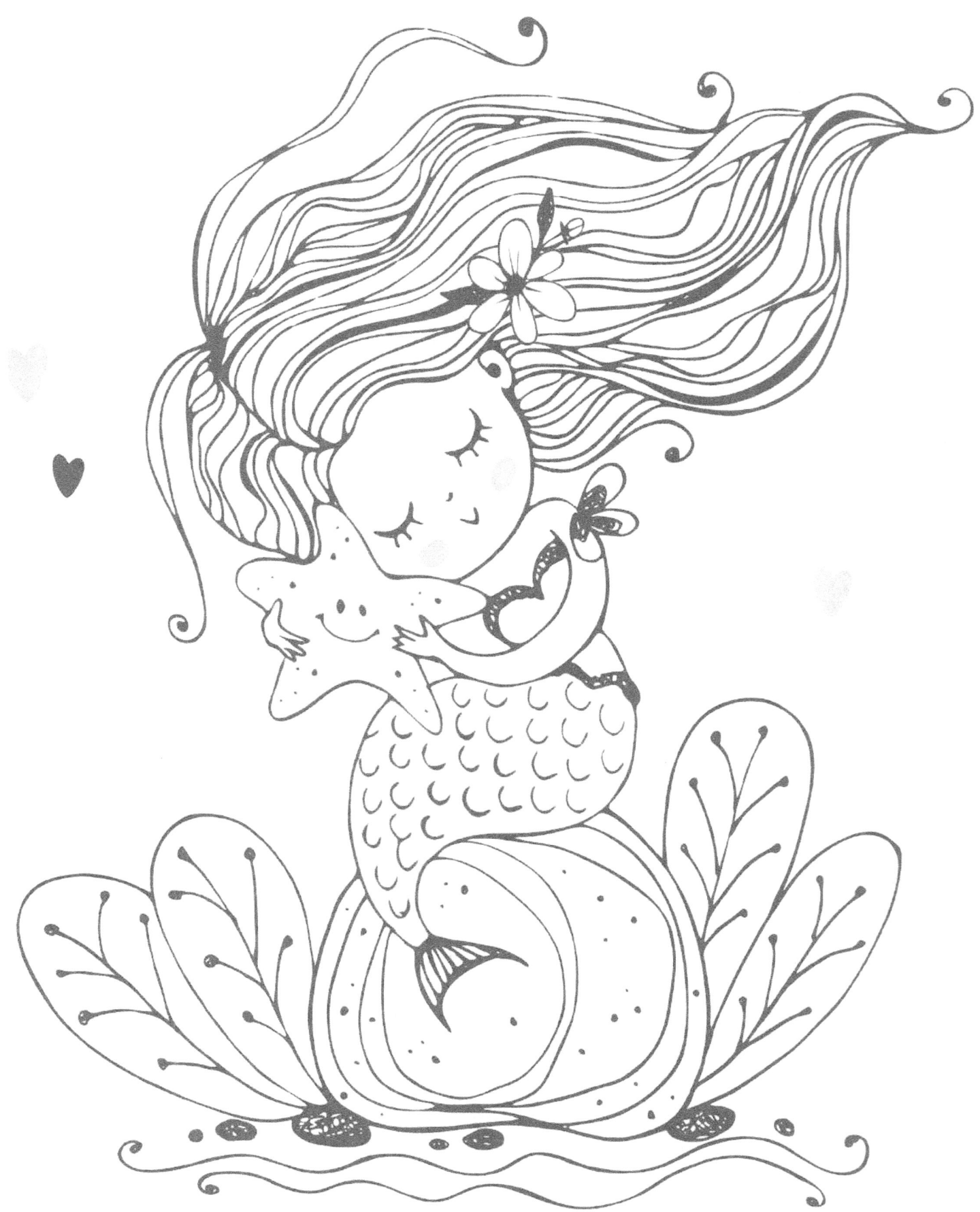

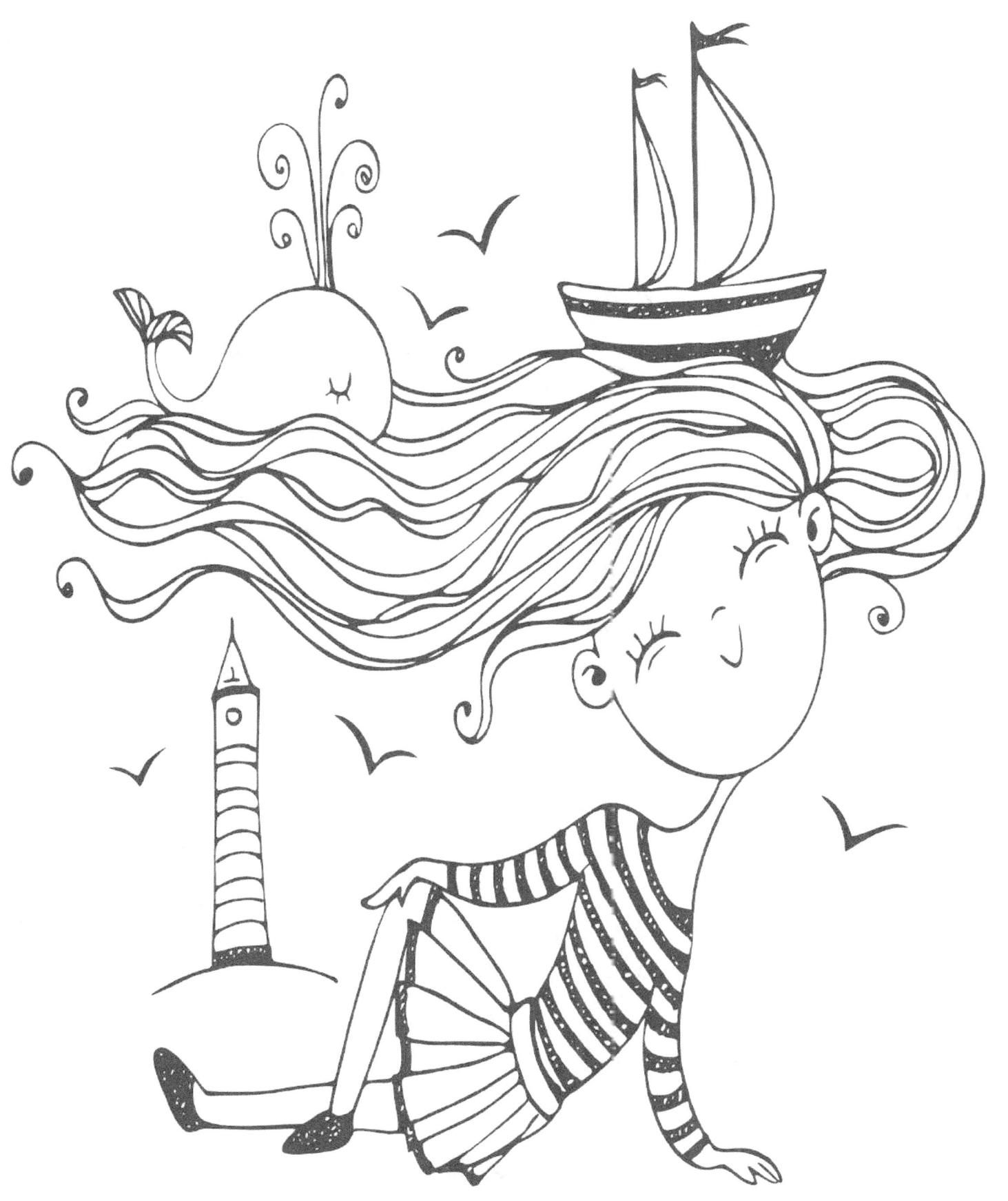

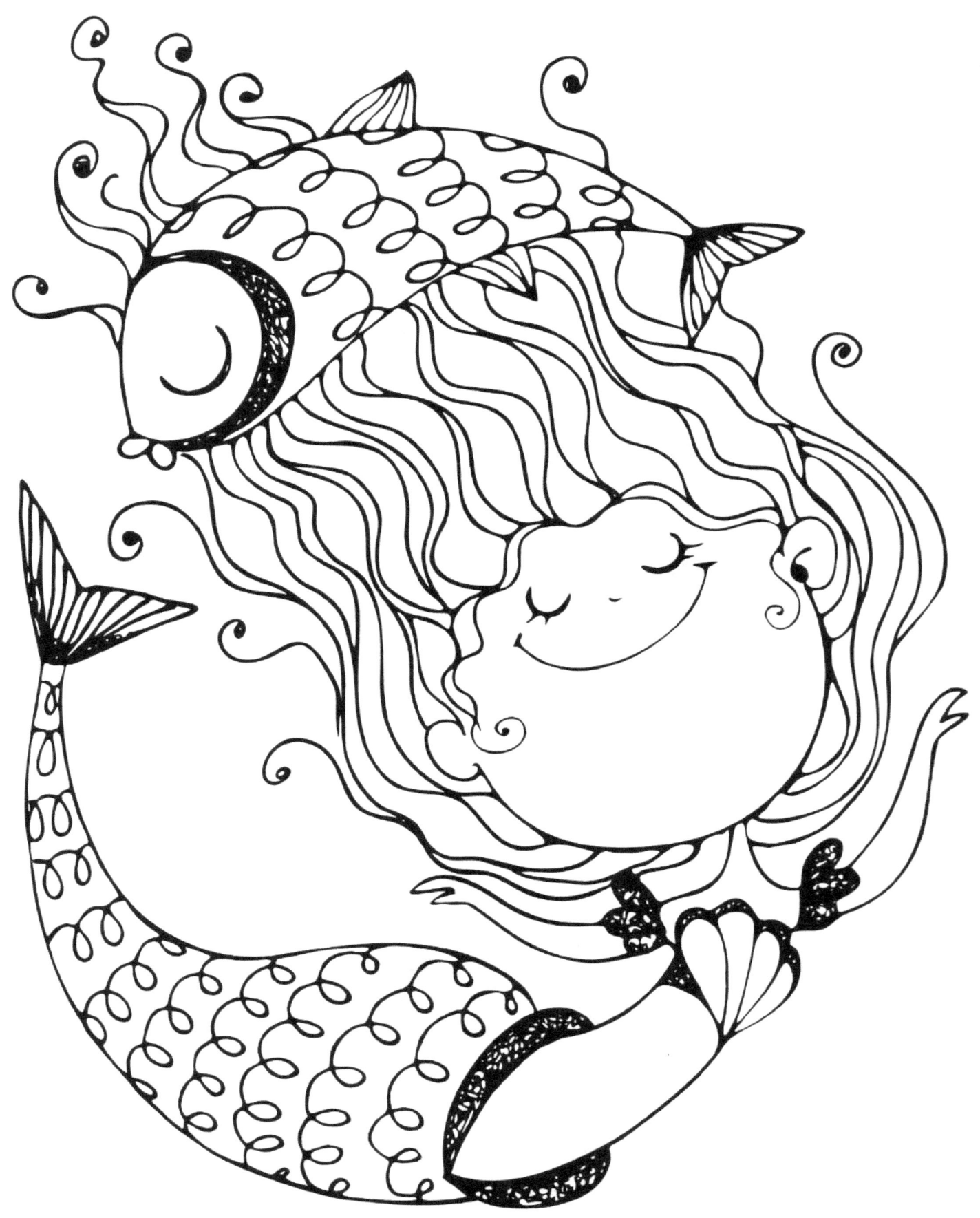

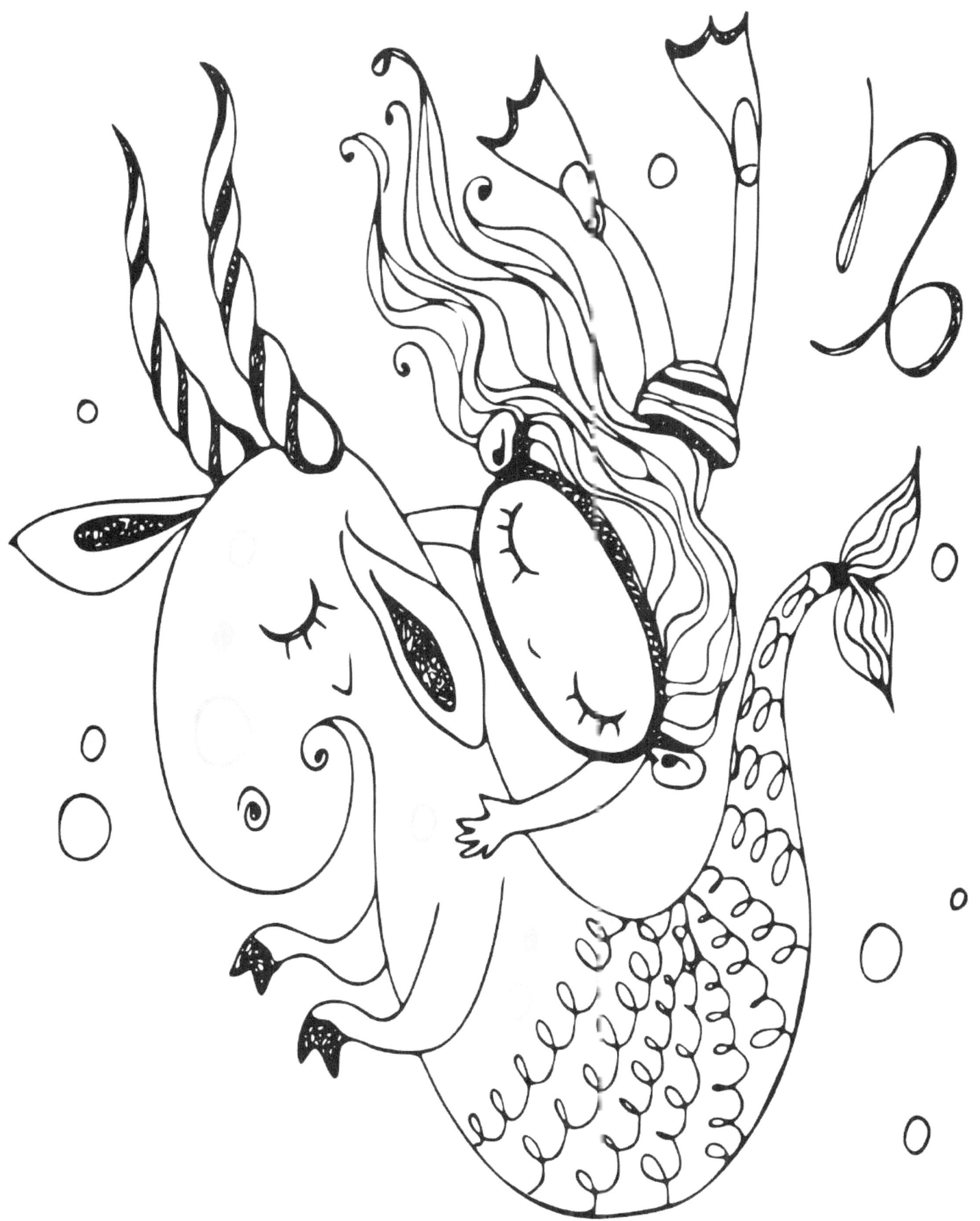

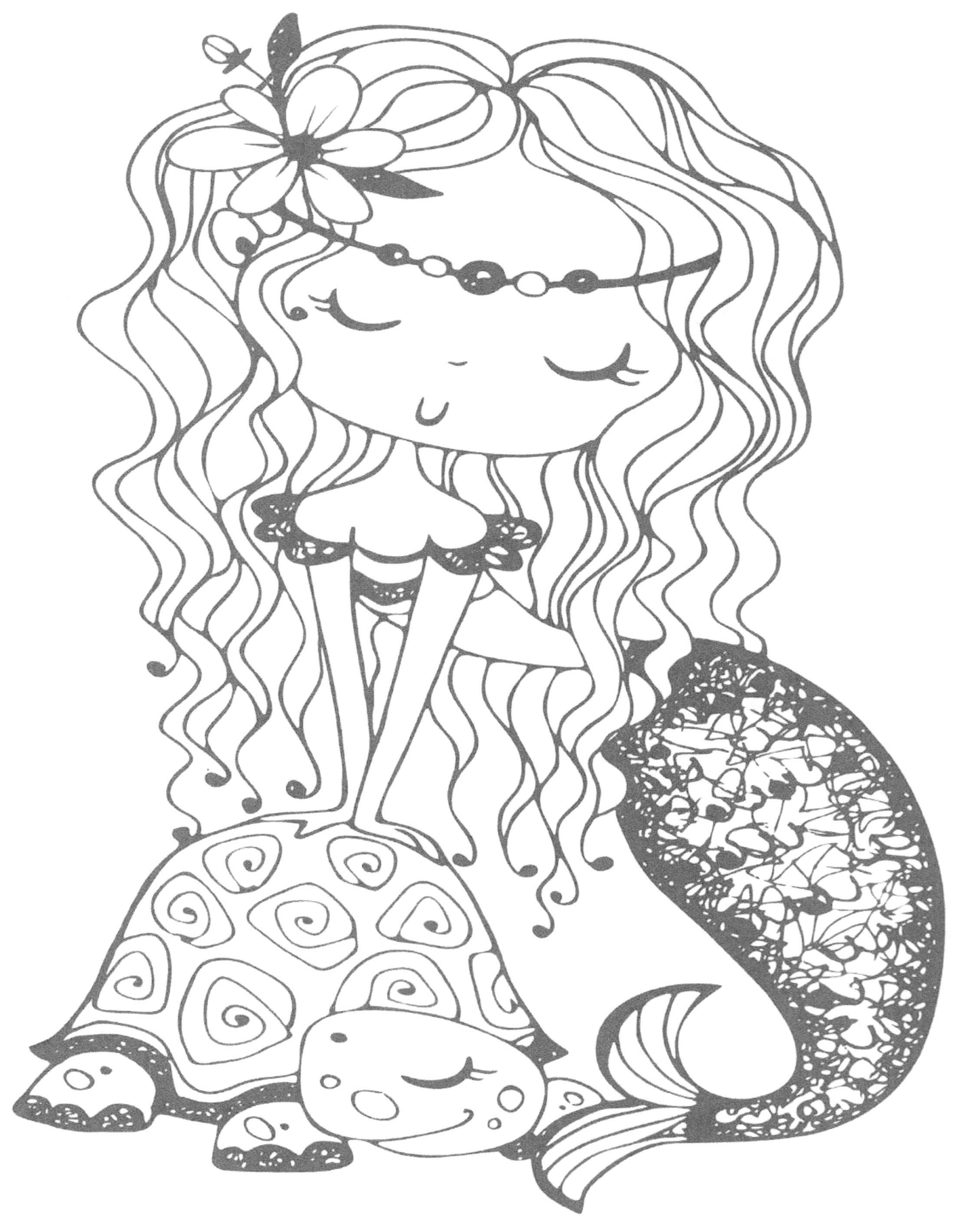

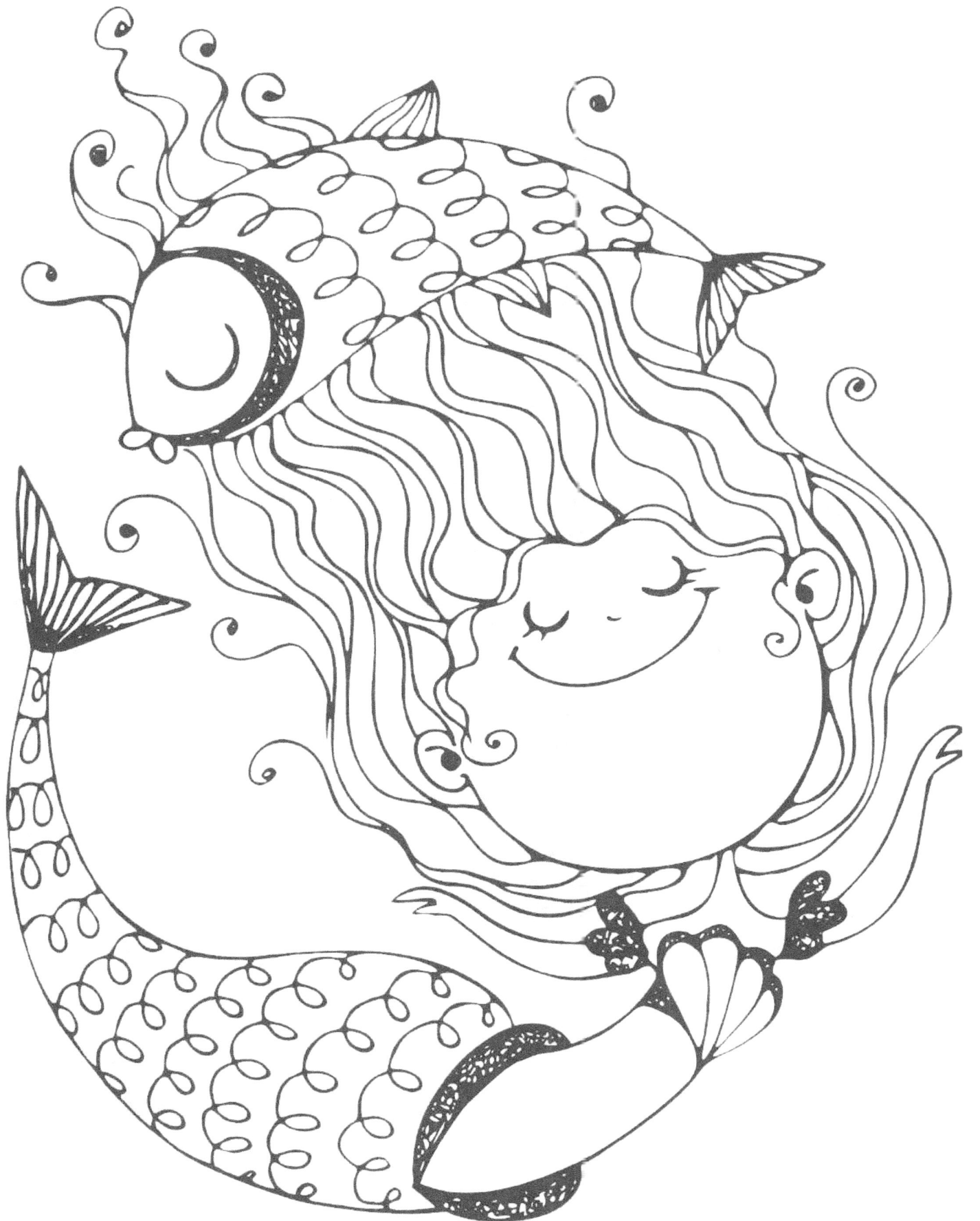

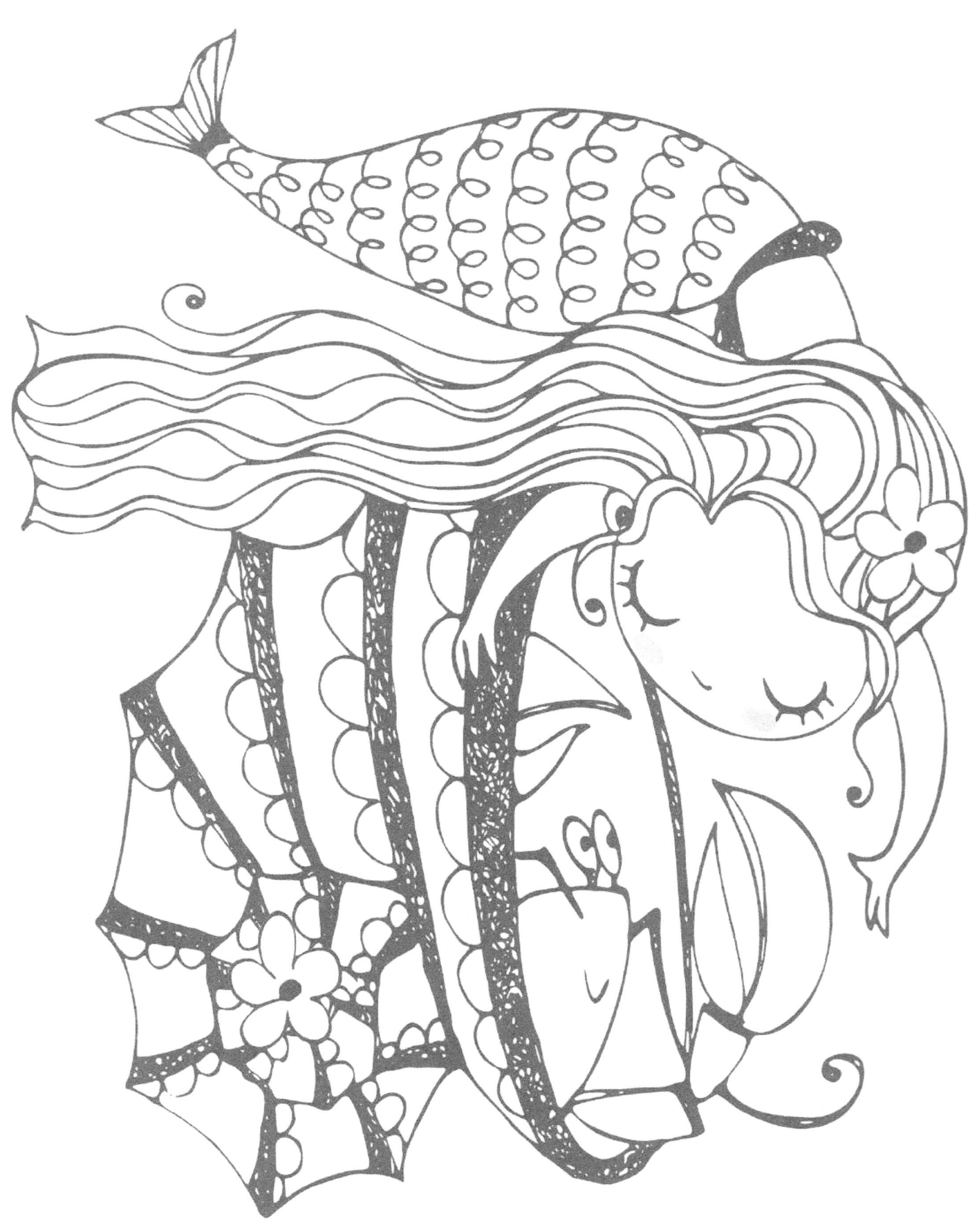

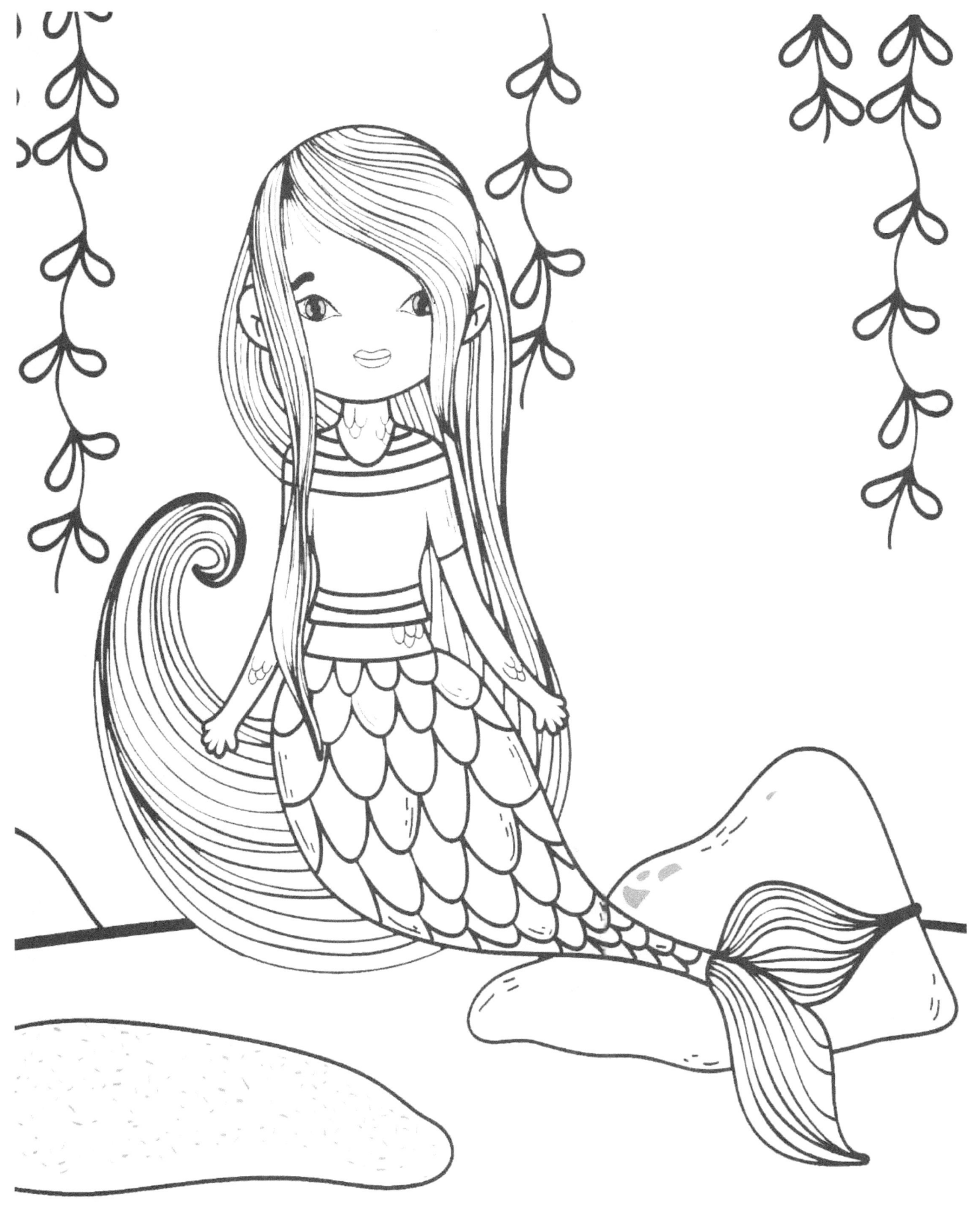

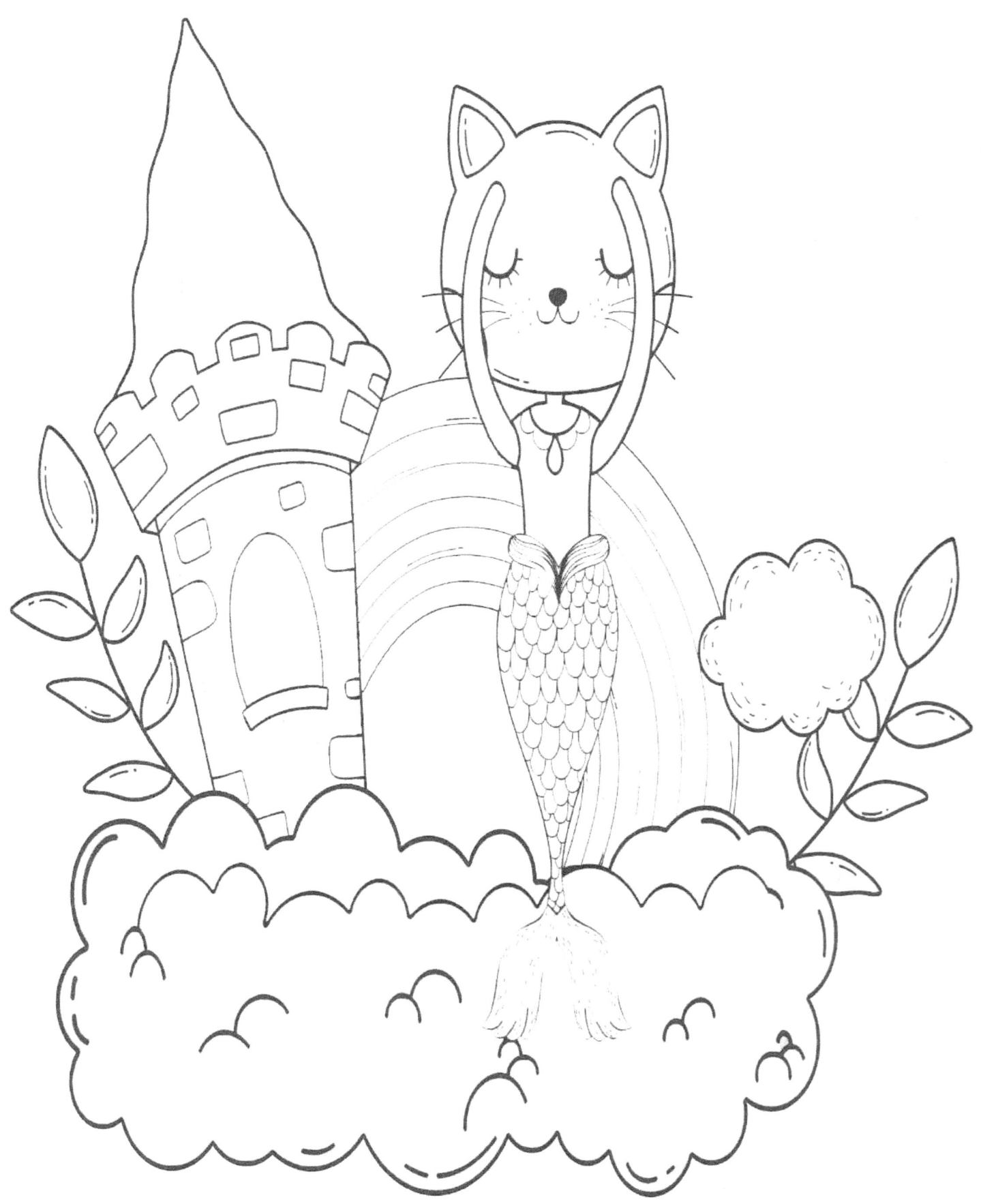

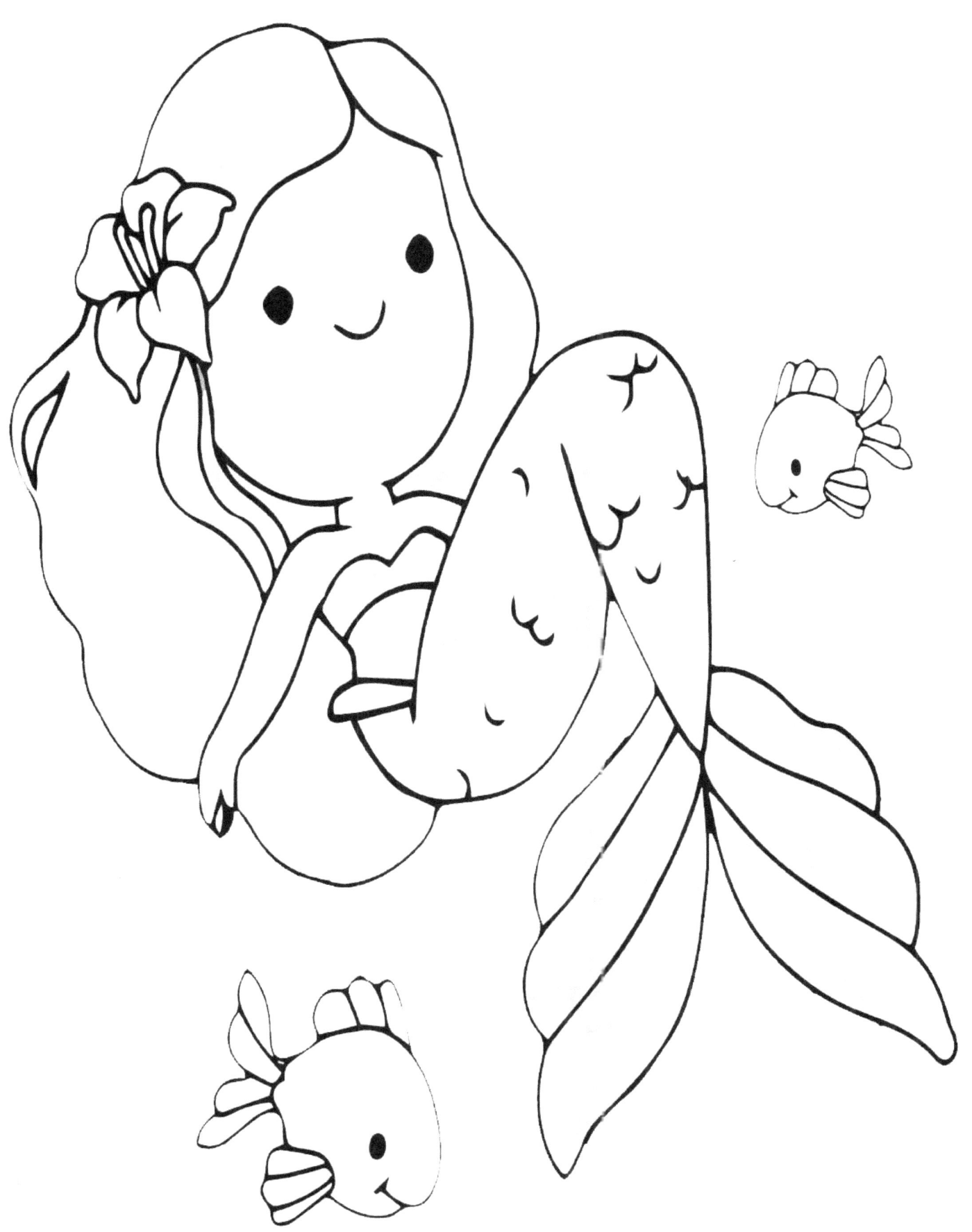

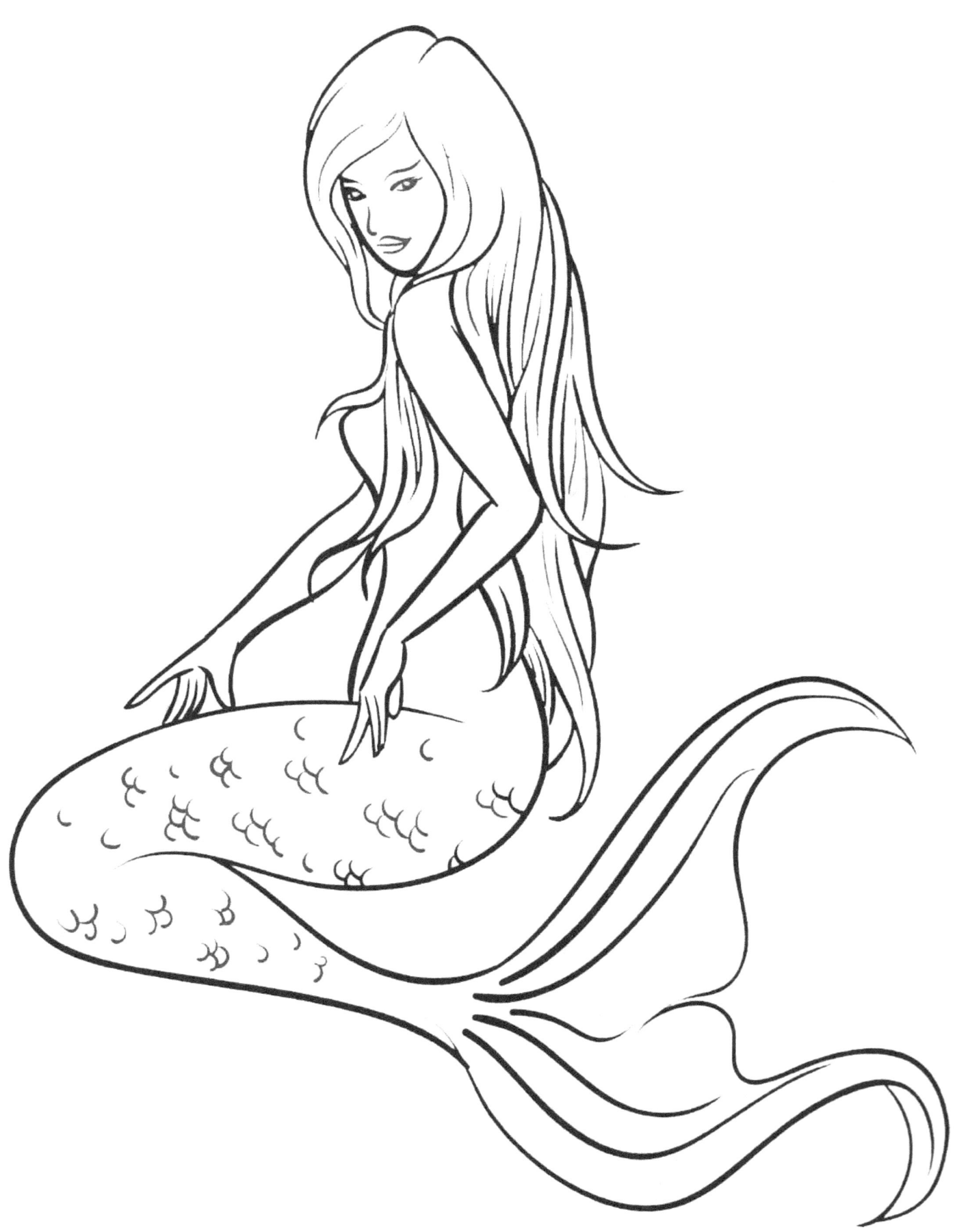

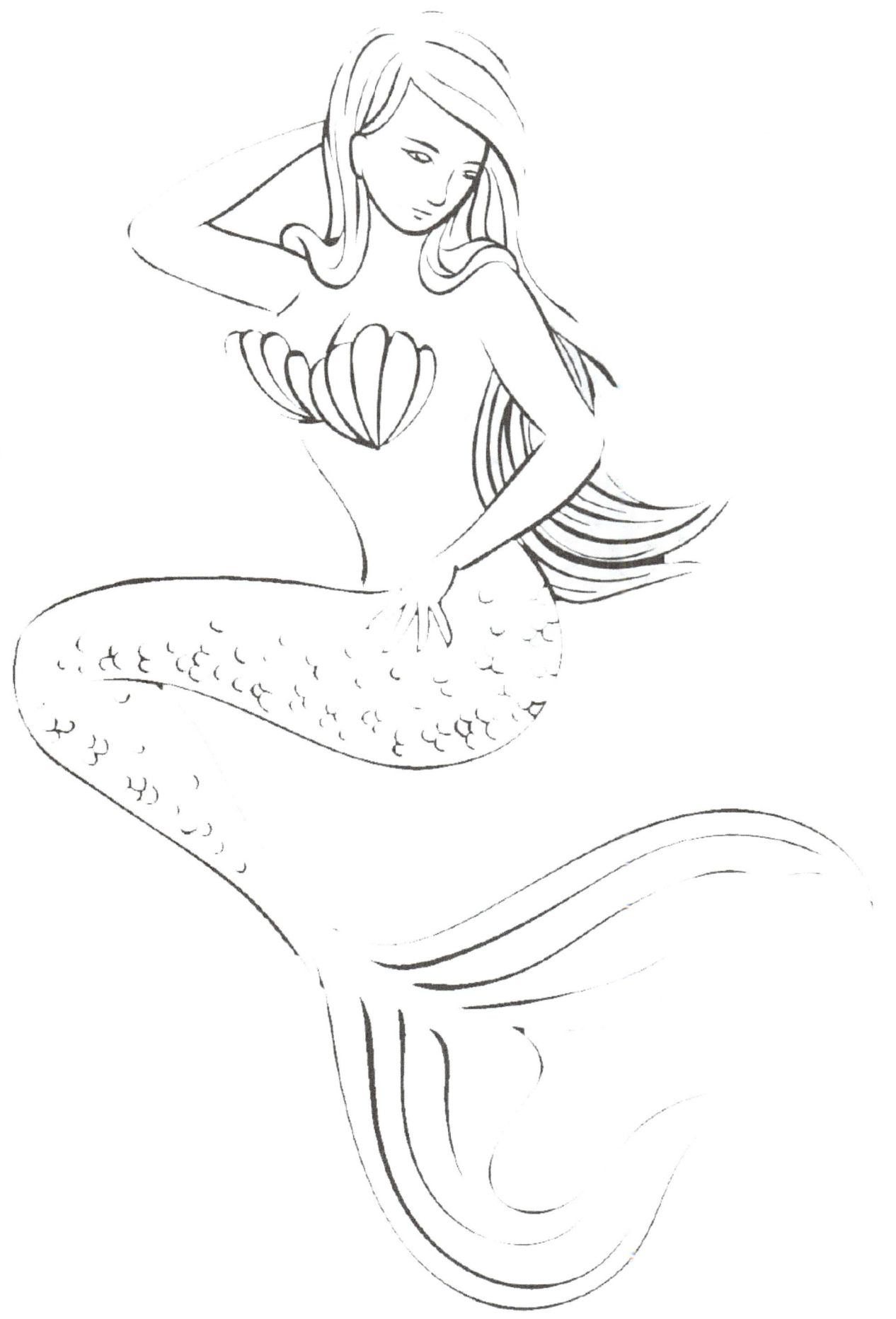

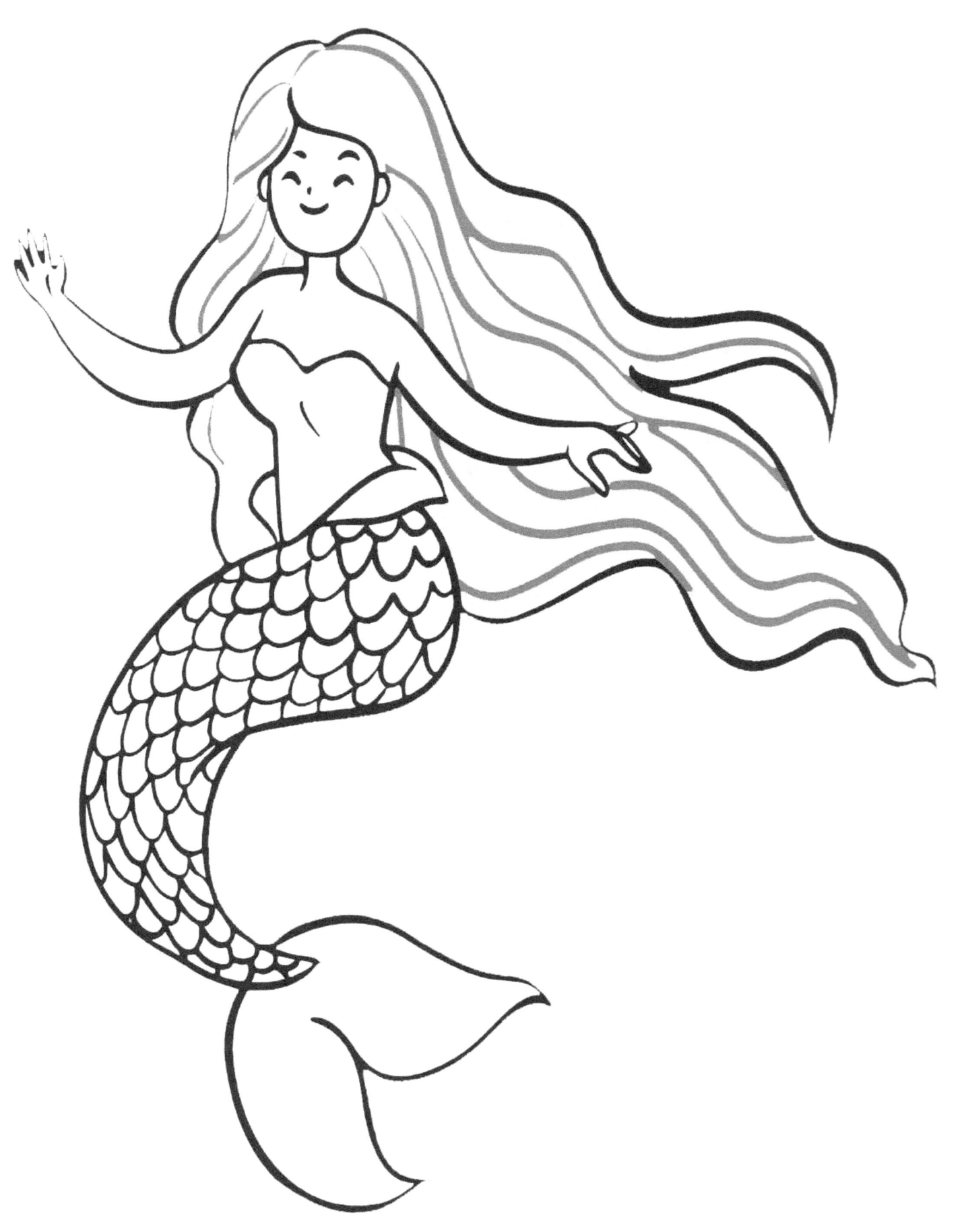

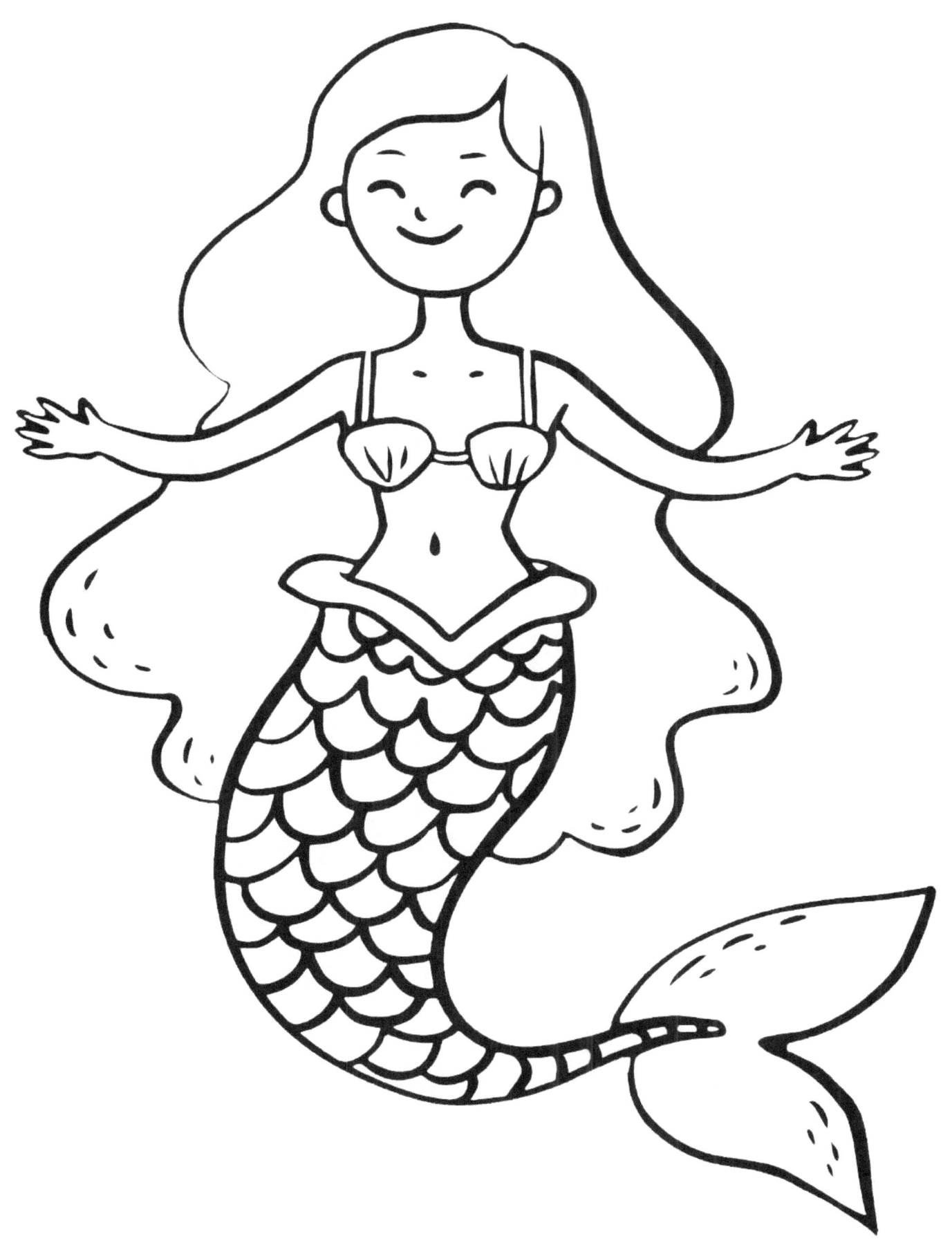

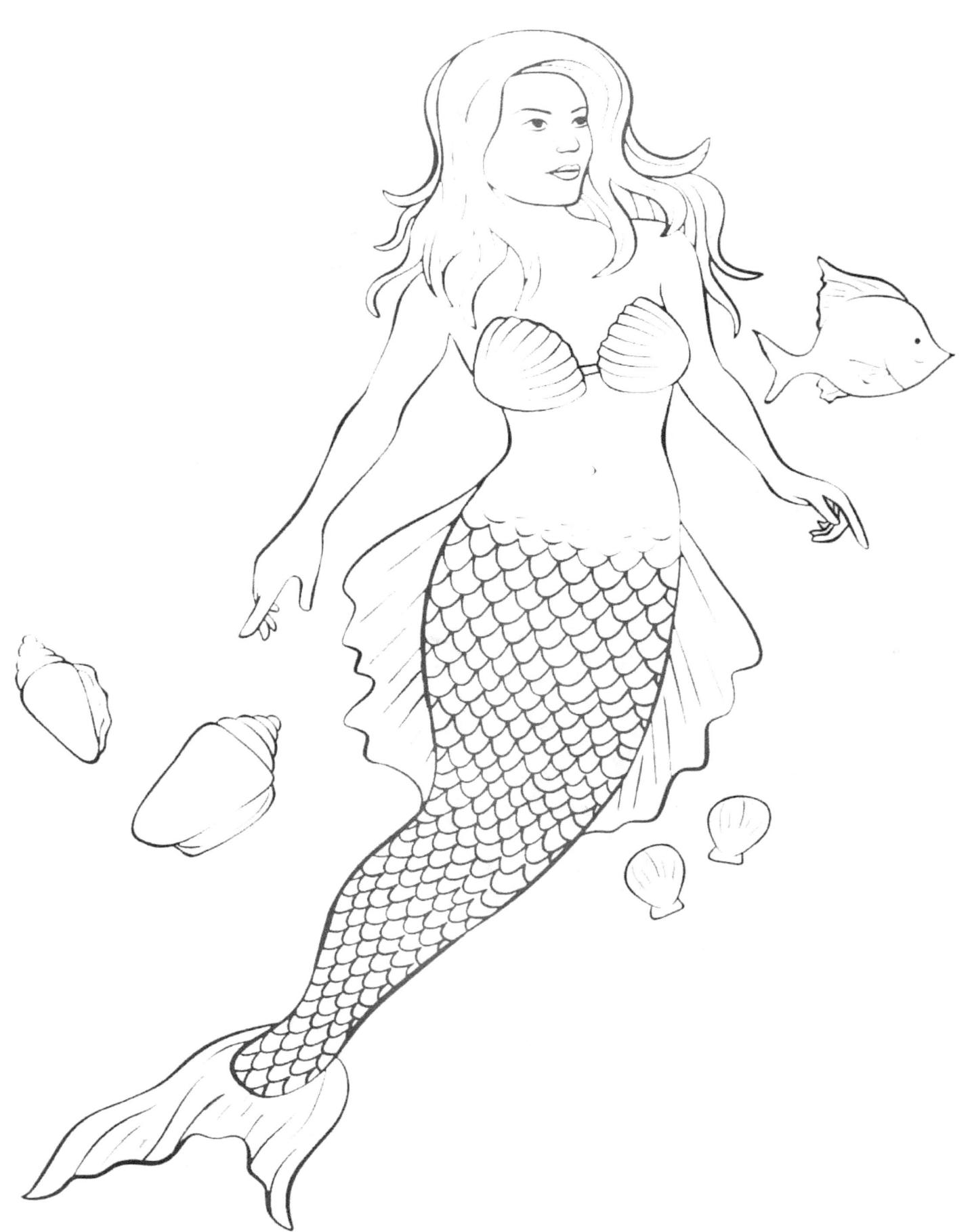

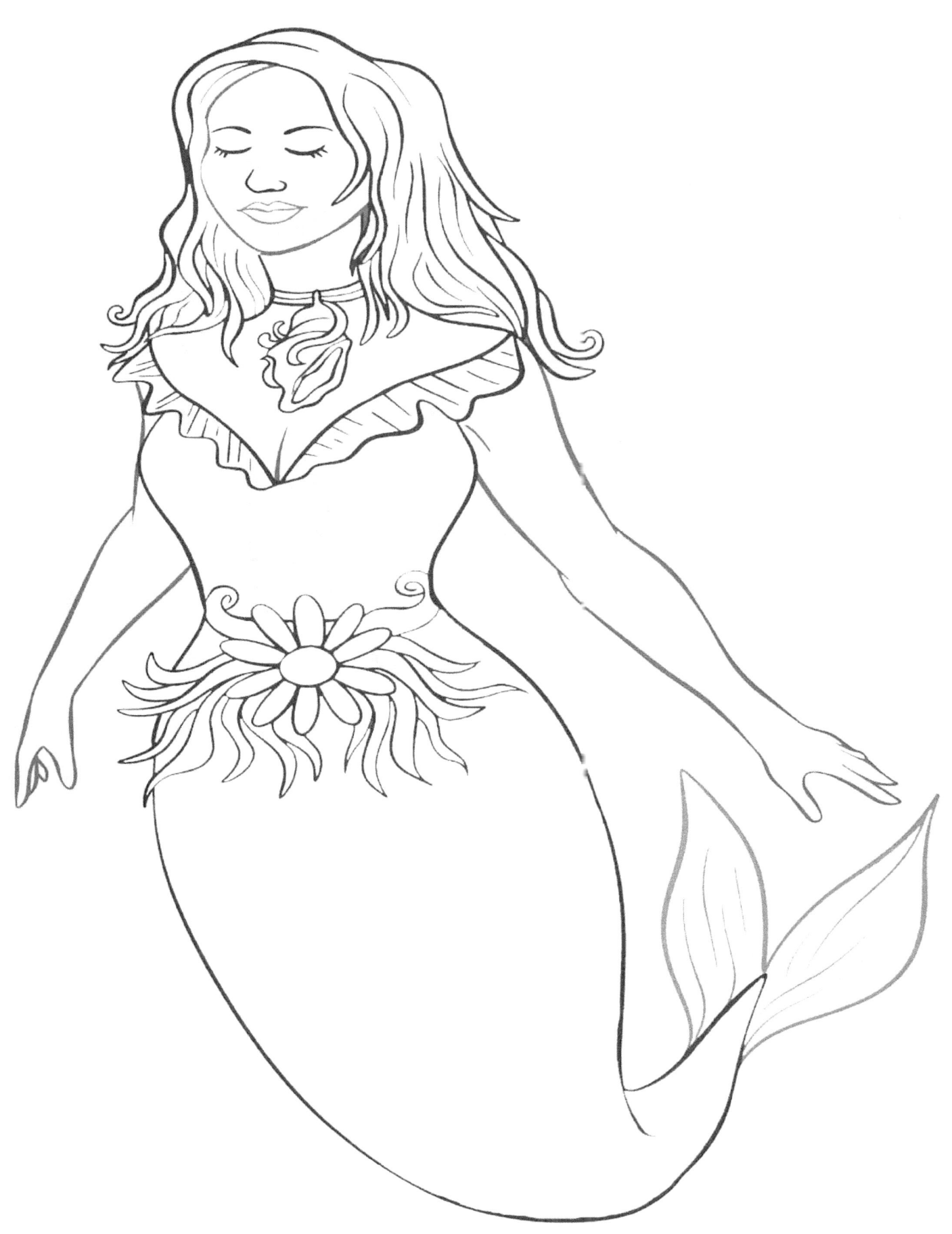

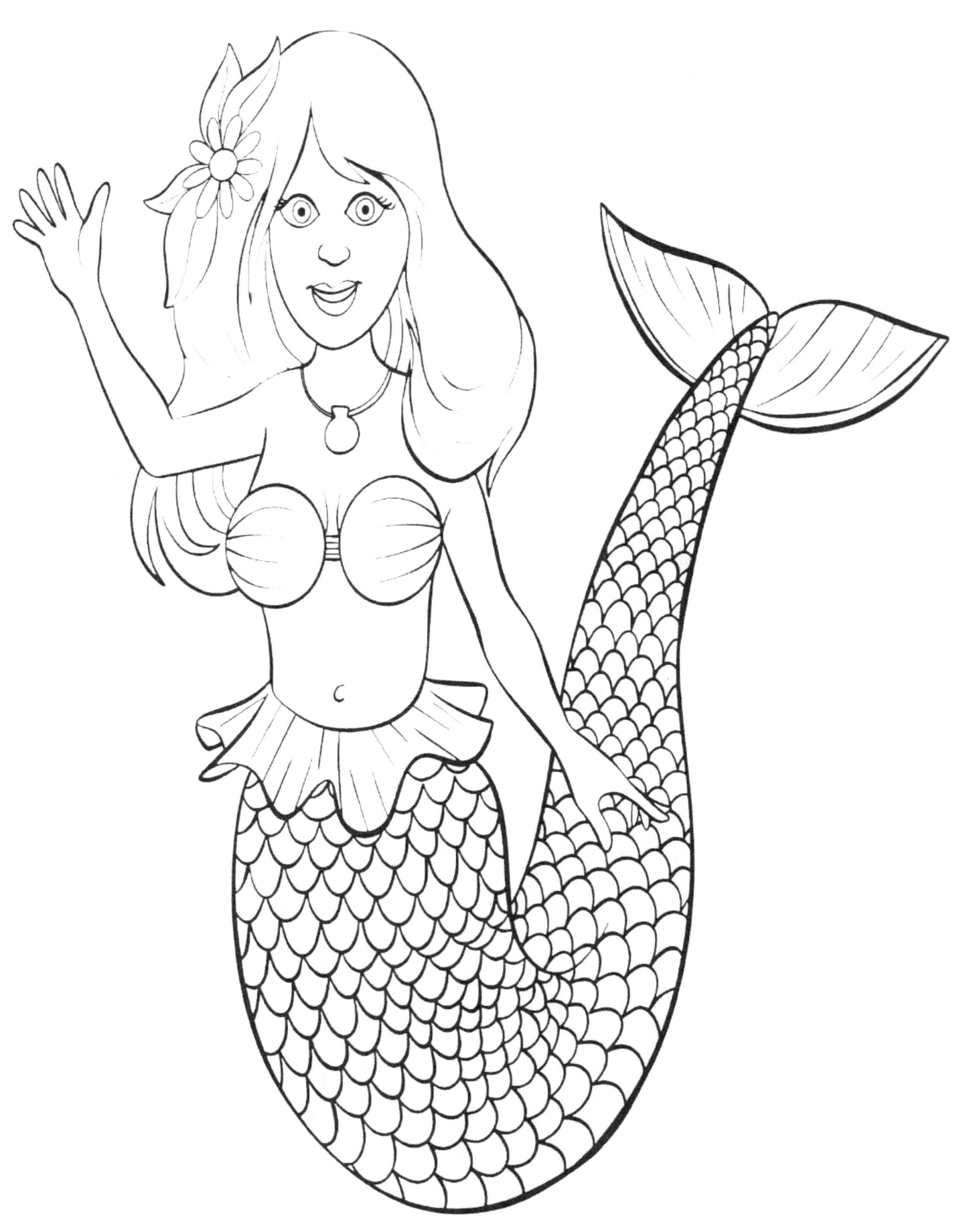

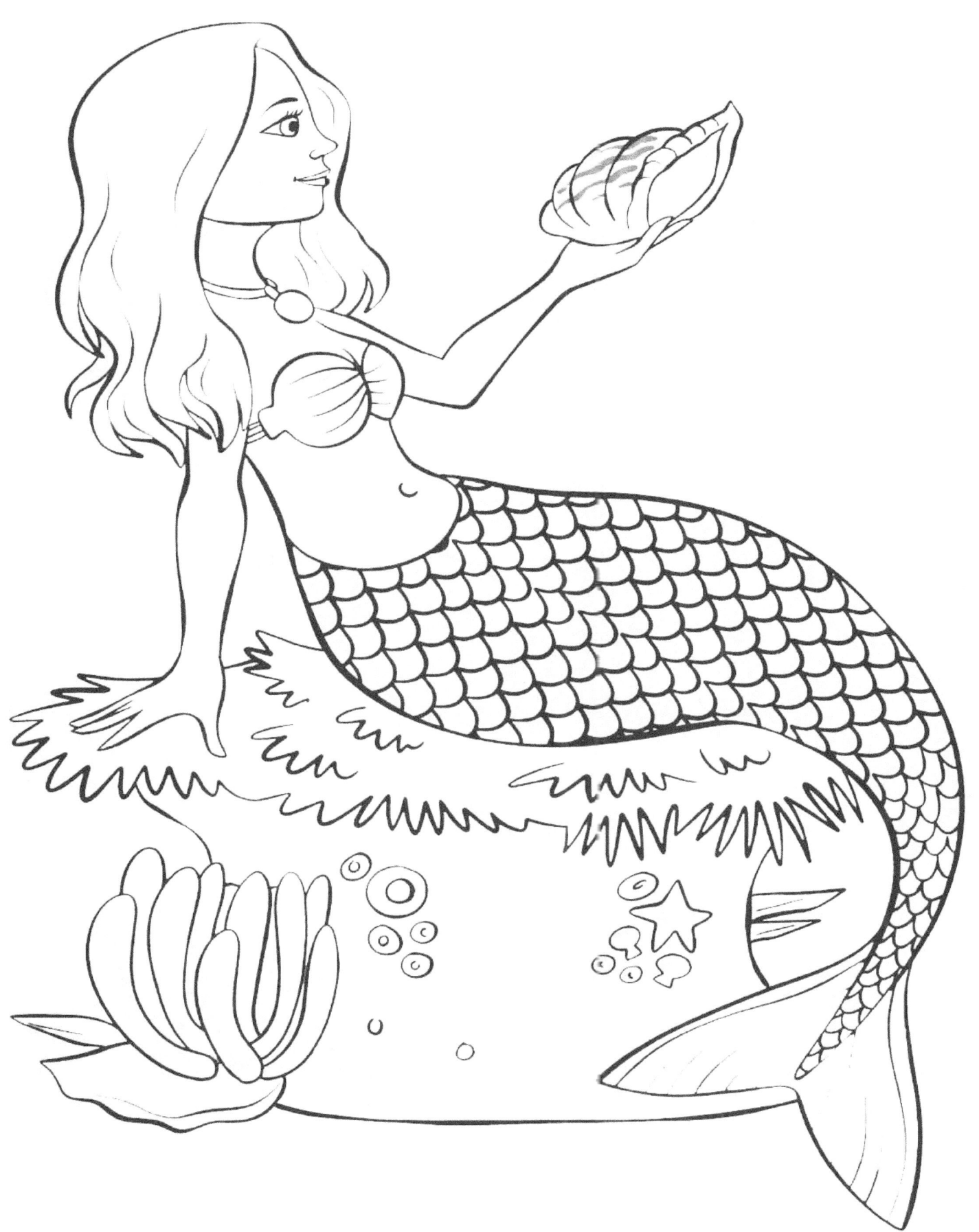

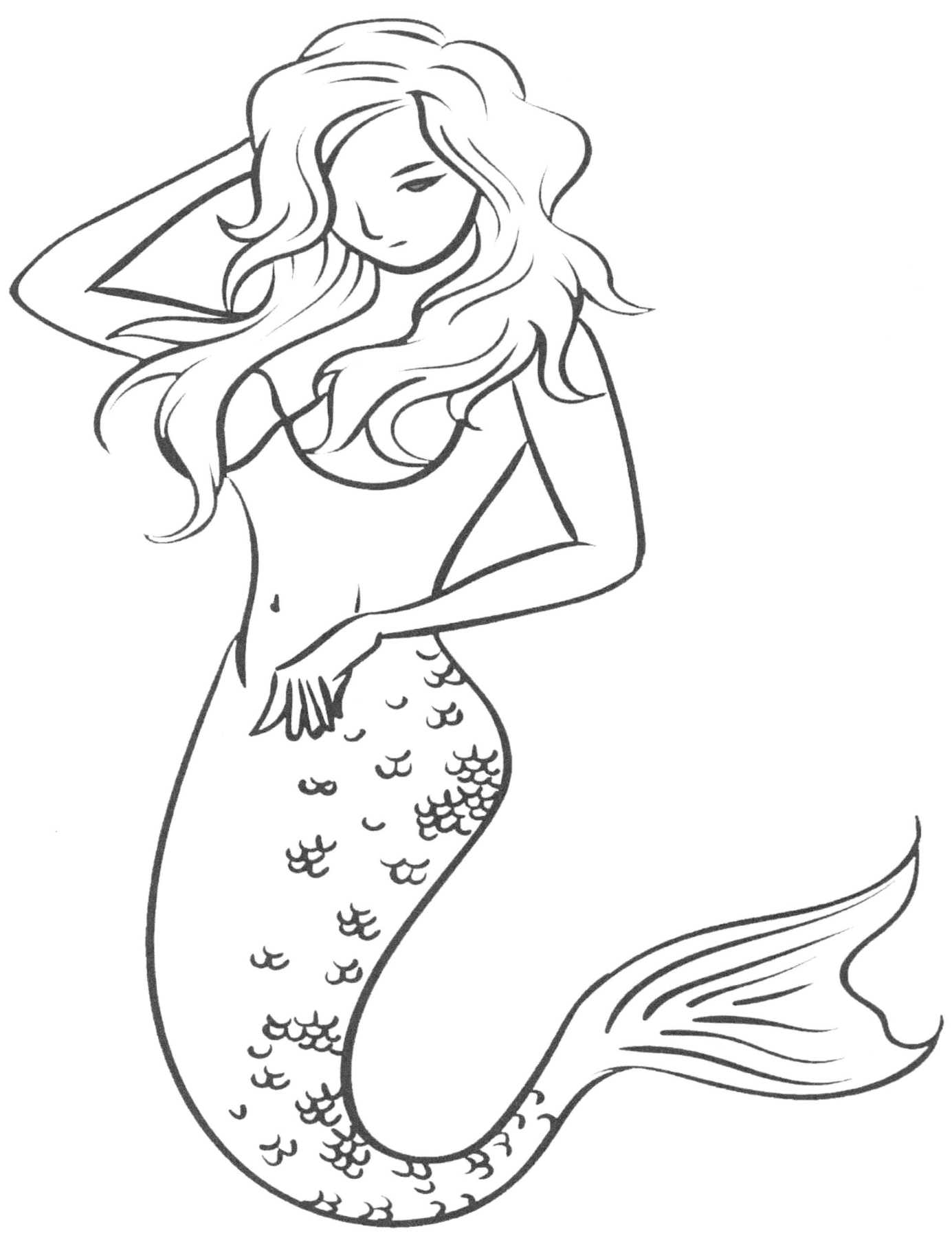

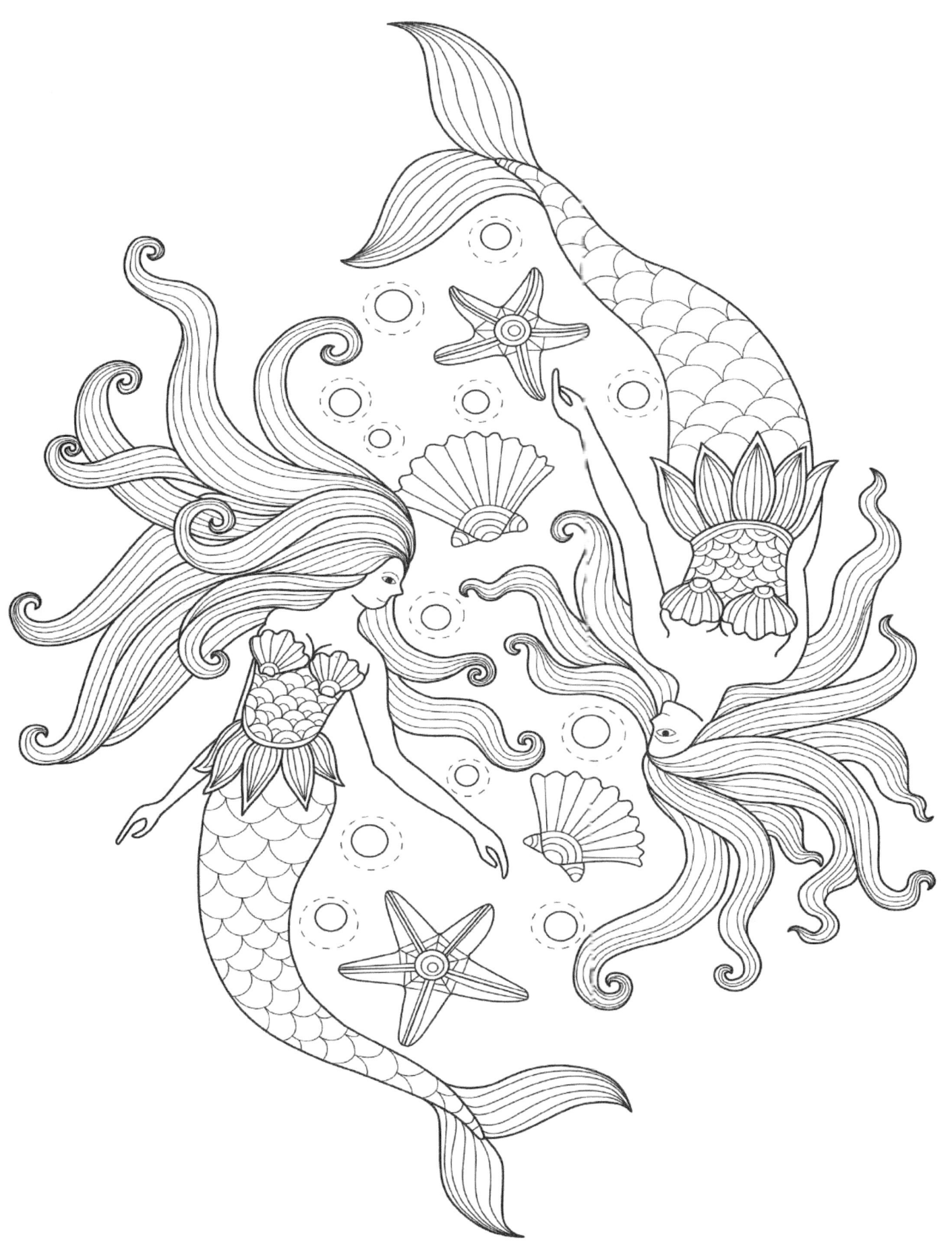

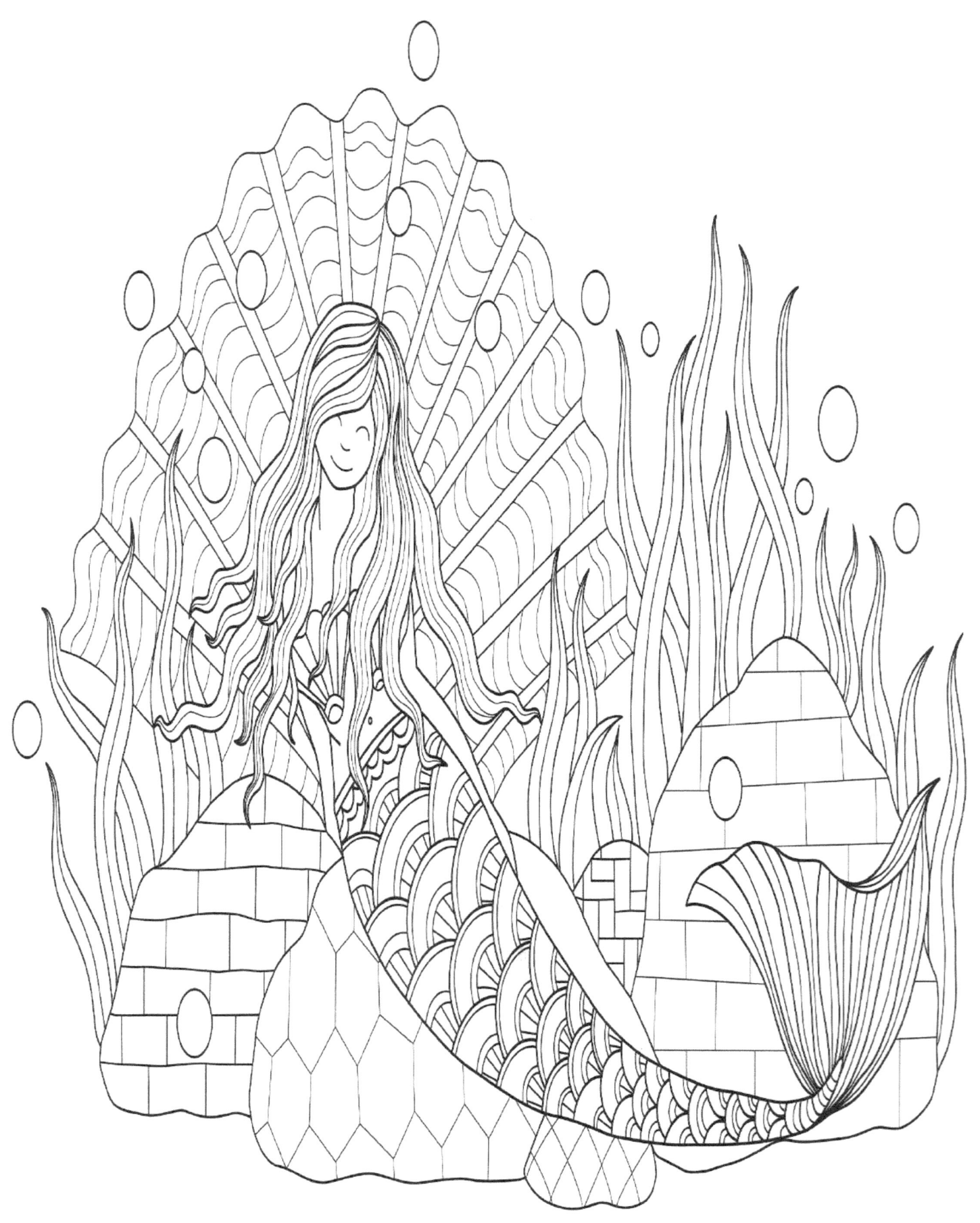

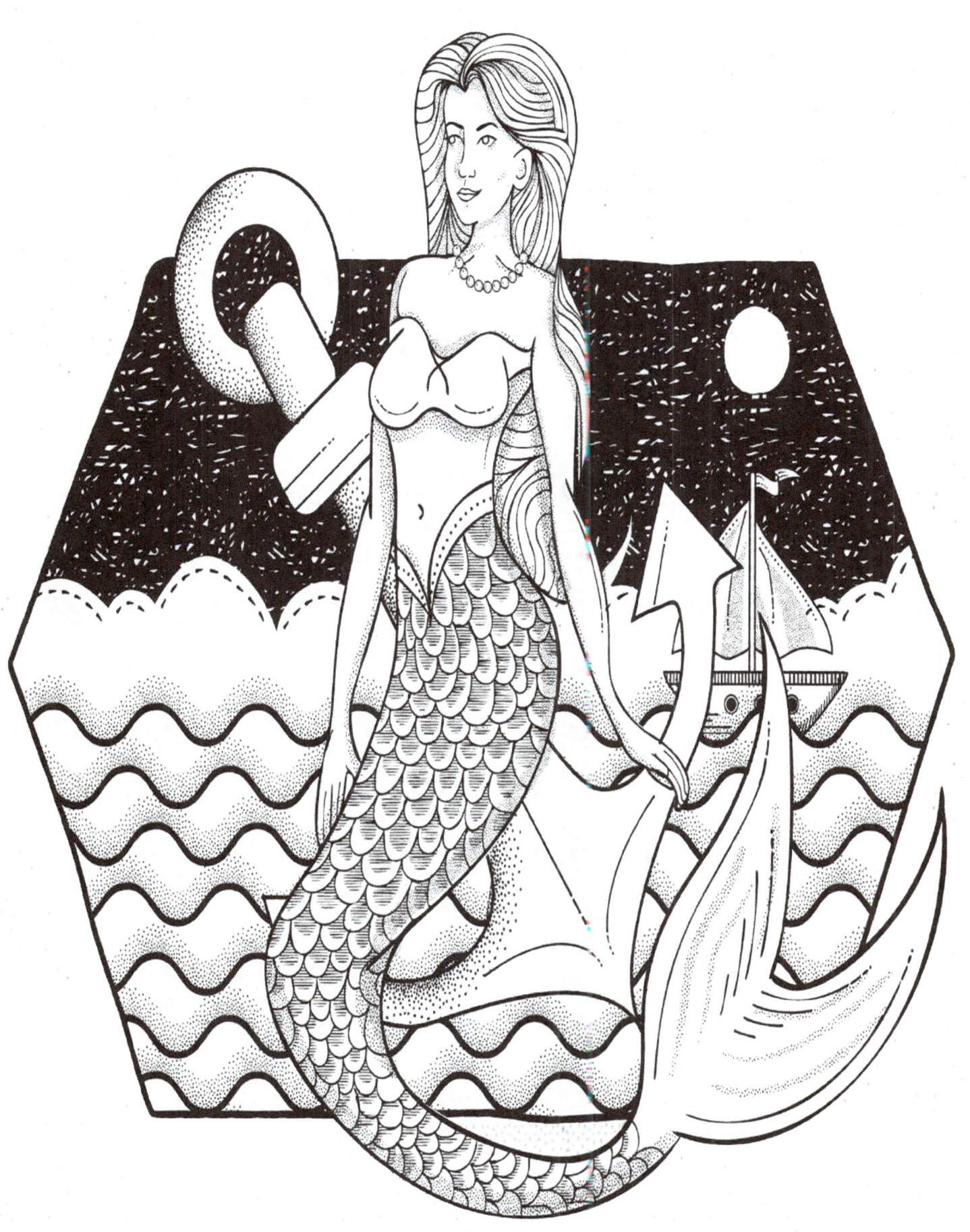

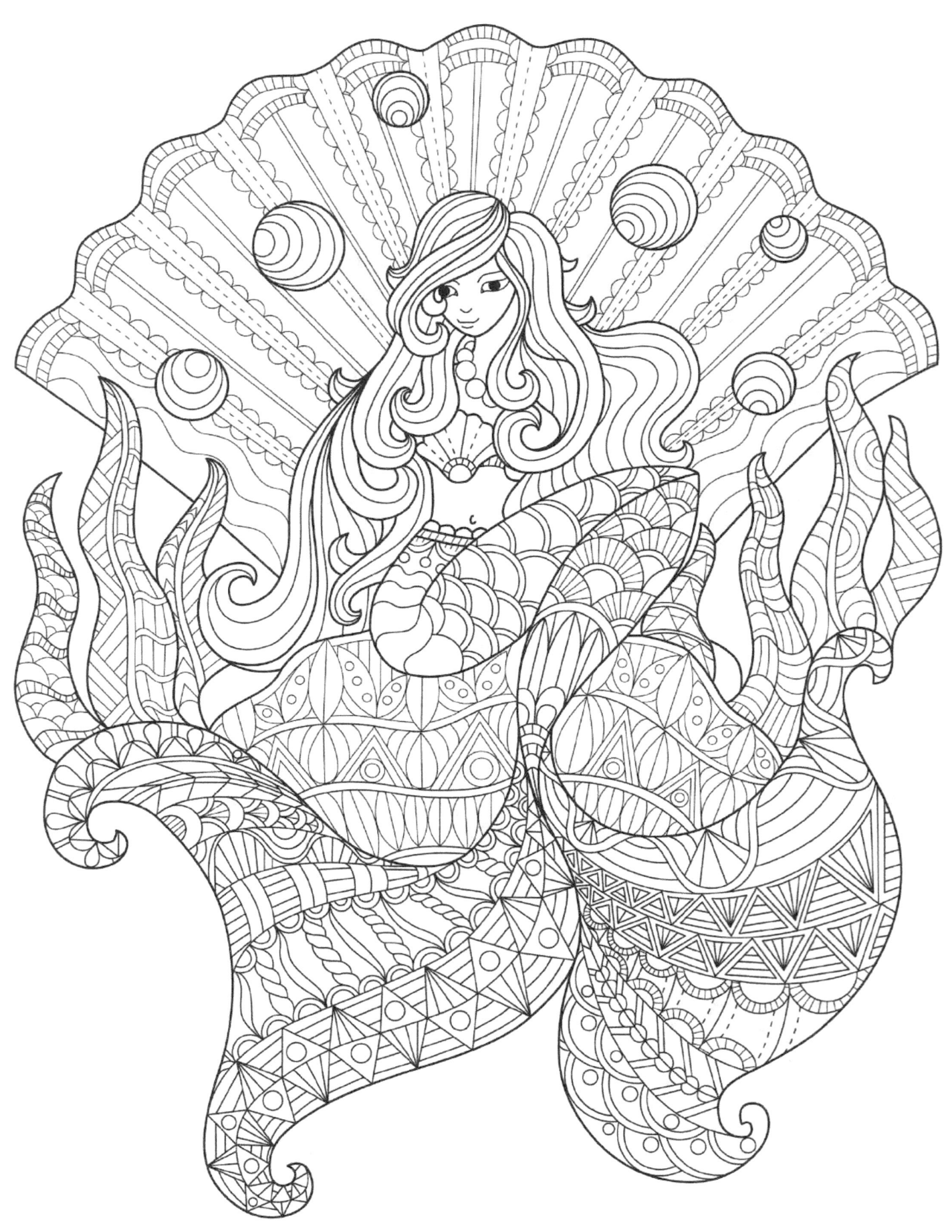

www.ingramcontent.com/pod-product-compliance
Lightning Source LLC
Chambersburg PA
CBHW060436220526
45465CB00008B/3160